LITTLE LADYSHIP

A Comedy in Three Acts

From the Hungarian of
Stefan Bekeffi and Adorjan Stella

by

IAN HAY

SAMUEL FRENCH LIMITED
LONDON

SAMUEL FRENCH, LTD.
26 SOUTHAMPTON STREET, STRAND, LONDON, W.C.2

SAMUEL FRENCH, INC.
25 WEST 45TH STREET, NEW YORK, U.S.A.
7623 SUNSET BOULEVARD, HOLLYWOOD 46, CAL.

SAMUEL FRENCH (CANADA), LTD.
480 UNIVERSITY AVENUE, TORONTO

MADE AND PRINTED IN GREAT BRITAIN BY
BUTLER AND TANNER LTD., FROME AND LONDON
MADE IN ENGLAND

The fee for the representation of this play by amateurs is Five Guineas, payable in advance to—

Messrs. Samuel French, Ltd.,
26 Southampton Street,
Strand, London, W.C.2,

or their authorized agents, who, upon payment of the fee, will issue a licence for the performance to take place.

No performance may be given unless this licence has been obtained.

In the event of further performances being given, the fee for each and every representation subsequent to the first is Four Guineas. This reduction applies only in the case of the performances being **consecutive** and at the **same theatre or hall.**

The following particulars are needed for the issue of a licence :

Title of the play(s).
Name of the town.
Name of the theatre or hall.
Date of the performance(s).
Name and address of applicant.
Name of the Society.
Amount remitted.

Character costumes and wigs used in the performance of plays contained in French's Acting Edition may be obtained from Messrs. CHARLES H. Fox, Ltd., 184 High Holborn, London, W.C.1.

LITTLE LADYSHIP

A COMEDY
by
IAN HAY

(Characters in order of their appearance)

HIGGINSON	*Iris Vandeleur.*
EVE	*Lilli Palmer.*
MRS. JESSUP	*Renee Kelly.*
MR. JESSUP	*Aubrey Mather.*
JUDY BINGLEY	*Joan White.*
SIR JOHN BRENT	*Cecil Parker.*
MRS. CYNTHIA BINGLEY	*Norma Varden.*
GRAVES (Sir John's Butler) . . .	*Sam Lysons.*
COLONEL BINGLEY	*Archibald Batty.*
MISS PHILPOTT (Headmistress of Tadworthy House)	*Elliot Mason.*
MISS MANDRILL (Assistant to Miss Philpott) .	*Beatrix Fielden-Kaye.*

HILDA SMITHSON		*Joan Ellum.*
CLAIRE WESTBROOK		*Phyllis Allan.*
OLIVE WAKEFIELD		*Dorothea Rodwell.*
AMY BATTERSBY		*Elspeth Cochrane.*
ANN WELLS	(Pupils at Tadworthy House School)	*Diana King.*
JANE HARDY		*Diana Barton.*
JOAN TIMPSON		*Joan Greenwood.*
HILDA HOBBS		*Lilian Williams.*
DAPHNE BROWNE		*Hilde Palmer.*

MERVYN BUDGE	*David Tree.*
SAMUEL SMITHSON	*Ernest Jay.*

Produced by GARDNER DAVIES.

Scenery and Decor by ERIC E. STERN.

The play was produced originally at The King's Theatre, Glasgow, on January 16th, 1939, and at the Strand Theatre, London, on February 7th of the same year.

SYNOPSIS OF THE ORIGINAL SCENERY

ACT I

SCENE 1.—Eve's Bedroom at Mr. Jessup's Flat.

SCENE 2.—Sir John Brent's House in Bryanston Square, London. The Lounge. Three months later.

ACT II

SCENE 1.—A Classroom at Tadworthy House School. A few weeks later.

SCENE 2.—Sir John Brent's House. The Lounge. Two days later.

ACT III

The Headmistress's Study at Tadworthy House. The next day.

SCENIC NOTE BY THE AUTHOR

" LITTLE LADYSHIP," as originally played, required four sets of scenery. For the sake of economy and ease in handling, I have now reduced the sets to three, and have, as far as possible, simplified their character, as follows :

ACT I, SCENE 1.—See stage directions on page 7 and ground plan on page 82.

ACT I, SCENE 2, ACT II, SCENE 2.—This was originally a large and elaborate set, with a massive staircase projecting on to the stage. This latter now only exists off stage. (See stage directions on page 19 and ground plan on page 83.) This scene should be made as roomy as possible, to permit of others being set inside it.

The third set now does double duty ; in ACT II, SCENE 1 as a classroom (see page 37 and ground plan on page 84), and in ACT III as a refreshment-room during the School Speech-day. All that is required is a change of furniture. Originally Act III was played in a fourth set —the Tadworthy Lodge drawing-room. This is now eliminated.

IAN HAY.

LITTLE LADYSHIP

ACT I

SCENE 1

SCENE.—EVE'S *bedroom in her parents' flat in Sloane Street. It is about 8.50 a.m. on a spring morning. It should be set, if possible, inside Scene 2, to save time in changing. A simpler arrangement would be to play the scene in front of a plain drop-curtain, using only the essential furniture, a bed, table and chair. The window and door could be treated as being just off* R. *and* L.

EVE *herself is in bed, completely covered by the bedclothes, which are spread right over the pillow. Underclothes and stockings are lying about untidily.*

Enter HIGGINSON, *an elderly maid and friend of the family. Then she looks at the bed and notes that the little morning tea-tray beside it has not been touched. She takes her stand above the bed.*

HIGGINSON. Miss Eve, may I inquire what's the use of bringing you a cup of tea with two lumps of sugar in the saucer, and pulling up that blind, if you just go on lying there? It'll be half-past nine presently, and then what will you look like? (*Crossing to the bed.*) It's you I'm talking to, Miss Eve. (C.) Miss Judy's here, in the car, and waiting for you. Do you want to be late for school?

(*She pulls back the bedclothes, revealing a pair of feet on the pillow;* EVE *is lying on her face, with her head down at the foot of the bed.*)

That's right; try and give me palpitations.

(*She pulls the clothes right down, revealing* EVE'S *head. She is a very pretty girl of eighteen, and wears pyjamas.*)

What do you want to go and do an upsetting thing like that for?

EVE (*turning over on her back*). Higgie darling, I'm dying. I must have crawled down here in a delirium or something. (*She gets into the proper position, and lies down again, on her left side, facing the audience.*)

HIGGINSON. What's the matter with you?

EVE. I don't know. Does it matter any more? Cover me up, please.

7

HIGGINSON. You were all right when you went to bed last night.

EVE. And I'm so *young* ! Pull down that blind, please.

HIGGINSON. I'll do no such thing !

EVE. You might as well ; you'll have to pull them all down presently.

HIGGINSON (*comes round below the bed*). Drink up your tea, and then pop into your slippers. (*She picks up the slippers and puts them together.*)

(EVE *shudders and moans.*)

(*Enter her mother,* MRS. JESSUP, *a brisk, middle-aged woman, who looks as if she would stand no nonsense. She is wearing a kimono.*)

MRS. JESSUP (C. *She picks up the clothes from the floor—puts the knickers on the chair, the rest in the drawers*). Eve, my dear child, aren't you up yet ? Do you know what time it is ? Your cousin Judy is waiting for you. Why isn't she up, Higginson ?

HIGGINSON. Because she's dying. (*She picks up a dress from the stool, crosses* L. *and hangs it in the cupboard.*)

MRS. JESSUP. Dying ? At this time of the morning ? Nonsense ! Go and turn her bath on—and see it's only *just* warm.

(*Exit* HIGGINSON L., *leaving the door open.*)

Now, Eve, what's the matter. (*She sits* L. *of the bed.*)

EVE. I've got double pneumonia, Mummy.

MRS. JESSUP. Don't be silly, dear. (*Feeling* EVE'S *forehead.*) You aren't even sticky. You were all right last night. Have you been guzzling chocolates in bed again ?

EVE. Please, please, don't talk about food—now !

MRS. JESSUP (*nodding*). I thought that was it ! Well, when you come home from school you shall go to bed after a plain supper, and have a nice dose of castor oil. That'll put you right.

(EVE *moans again.*)

(*She picks up the dressing-gown and crosses* L. *to the wardrobe.*) The pity of it is we didn't send you to a boarding-school ! That's your mollycoddle of a father again !

EVE. I want to see a doctor, please !

(*Enter* MR. JESSUP, L.—*a rather fussy, bald-headed man, in a dressing-gown. His face is covered with lather, and he has a shaving-brush in his hand and a towel round his neck.*)

MR. JESSUP (*running to the bed*). Eve, my dear child, what is the matter ? Tell your old father ! What is it ? (*He kisses* EVE, *leaving soap on her face.*)

MRS. JESSUP (*caustically*, L.).   She doesn't require a shampoo, anyhow.

MR. JESSUP.   Bertha, don't be callous! (*He tenderly wipes EVE's face.*)   What's the matter, dear?

EVE.   Daddy, I'm feeling awful.

MR. JESSUP.   There, there! (*He feels EVE's forehead.*)   The child is in a raging fever.

MRS. JESSUP.   The child has got a stomach-ache.   I am taking steps.

EVE (*angrily*).   I haven't got a stomach-ache.   I've—I've got —appendicitis.

MR. JESSUP.   I must take her temperature at once!   Where's the thermometer?

MRS. JESSUP (L.).   In your dressing-room top drawer, as usual.

MR. JESSUP.   At once, at once!

(*Exit* MR. JESSUP *up* L.)

MRS. JESSUP (*crosses to* C.).   Eve, are you quite sure you're not shamming?

EVE.   Daddy doesn't think so.   He understands!

MRS. JESSUP.   He understands nothing about anything, and never did, and he spoils you ridiculously. (*She helps* EVE *up in bed.*)   All the same, this isn't quite like you.   I must say you're usually up with the lark, and nothing keeps you away from school as a rule.   Judy says the girls in your class call you Queen Sap, whatever that may mean.   Now, if I were Judy's mother, and Judy were to wake up dying at this hour of the morning, I should know exactly what was the matter with her, and what to do about it.

JUDY (*off stage* L.).   Still in bed?

(*Enter* EVE's *young cousin*, JUDY, *dressed for school.*)

MRS. JESSUP.   Oh, here she is.

JUDY.   Hallo!   Why isn't Goggie up? (*To* EVE.)   You'll be late for school, teacher's pet, and then what? (*She jumps on the lower side of* EVE's *bed.*)

EVE.   Don't do that! (*She rolls over and moans.*)

JUDY (*to* MRS. JESSUP).   What's the matter with her?   Going to have twins, or something?

MRS. JESSUP.   Judy! (*Down stage.*)

(JUDY *jumps over the bed—sits on the stool* R.)

(*Enter* MR. JESSUP *hurriedly, with a thermometer.   He sits on the chair* L. *of the bed and gives his wife the razor.*)

MR. JESSUP.   Here's the thermometer. (*To* EVE.)   Open your mouth, darling.   It'll all be over in a minute now.

EVE.   Will you send for the doctor, *please*, Daddy?

Mrs. Jessup. No !

Mr. Jessup. Yes, dear ; but let me take your temperature first. Open—close ! Don't bite it ! There ! (*He puts the thermometer into her mouth and sits watching her anxiously.*)

(Mrs. Jessup *hands him the razor.*   Judy *holds up the mirror.*)

(*Enter* Higginson, l.)

Higginson (l.).   Your bath's ready, Miss Eve.

Mr. Jessup (*rises*).   Bertha, the child can't possibly have a bath if she has a temperature.

Mrs. Jessup (*up* l.).   And as she hasn't a temperature she can have a bath.

Mr. Jessup (*up in the doorway*).   I am going to ring up Dr. Mackenzie at once.

Mrs. Jessup. And you'll find he is in Scotland, fishing in the Dee, or the Don——

Judy.   Or the Dnieper, or the Dniester, or the Bug——

Mr. Jessup. Well, there's a locum. Mackenzie always leaves a number we can ring up if he's going away. Where is it ?

Mrs. Jessup. Somewhere on that pad beside the telephone. But must we ?

Mr. Jessup.   Of course we must. I do hope he's a reliable man. (*He picks up the pad.*)   Is this it ?

Mrs. Jessup. I expect so. I must finish dressing, even if it is a locum.

(*Exit* Mrs. Jessup, *leaving* Mr Jessup *to dial a number.*)

(*During this conversation* Judy *has edged close to her uncle and aunt to overhear what they are saying.* Eve *seizes the opportunity to remove the thermometer from her mouth and hold it in her tea ; then puts it back.* Judy *turns suddenly and sees her.* Judy *goes to the chest of drawers up* c., *takes* Eve's *bag and takes out a coin.*)

Eve (*mumbling with the thermometer in her mouth*).   What are you doing ?

Judy.   I'm blackmailing you, darling. There's a shilling here I can use.

Eve (*sits up*).   What do you mean ?

Judy. I saw you swoshing that thermometer round in your tea. What's the game ?   (*She throws the bag back.*)

(Eve *closes her eyes and moans.* Mr. Jessup *has now got the number, and speaks.*)

Mr. Jessup.   Hullo !   Hullo !   (*Down* l.)   This is Mr. Jessup, Flat Seven, Wilton House, Sloane Street. Could the doctor come round here at once, please ? Yes, yes. Will you bring the doctor to the telephone ?   I must speak to him in person.

JUDY. It isn't like you to try to get off school. Are you in a jam over something ? I simply can't believe it : you're too pure. Now, if it was me——

MR. JESSUP. Yes, it's extremely urgent. What ? Well, I'm sure you'll make an exception in this case. It's my daughter . . . (*His voice goes into a mumble.*)

JUDY. I'll get it out of you sooner or later, you know. And if it's anything really juicy, my tariff for silence may go up. (*She crosses* R. *to the dressing-table, picking up a scent-bottle from the dressing-table.*) You wouldn't like to give me this scent-spray, I suppose ?

EVE. No, I wouldn't. (*Warming up the thermometer again in her tea.*) You'd better get out of here, Judy, you'll be late for school.

JUDY. It's only just after nine. (*She picks up a scarf.*) This might put me in an indulgent mood.

EVE (*emphatically*). Will you——?

MR. JESSUP (*hangs up the telephone*). It's all right ! It's all right ! The doctor is on his way, my dear. He made quite a fuss about coming. I can't think why ! (*Taking the thermometer from* EVE's *mouth and examining it.*) Good heavens ! A hundred and two !

EVE. I knew it ! I knew it !

MR. JESSUP (*calling*). Bertha ! Bertha !

(MRS. JESSUP *enters from the bedroom and comes* L. *of him.*)

(*Showing the thermometer.*) A hundred and two !

MRS. JESSUP. Stuff and nonsense ! (*Looking at the thermo-meter.*) A hundred and two ! Hm ! Have you sent for the doctor ?

MR. JESSUP. Yes.

MRS. JESSUP. What is his name ?

MR. JESSUP. I don't know. There was nothing on the pad but his telephone number, and I didn't like to ask him. (*Crossing to* EVE *and sitting on the chair by her bed.*) How do you feel now, my dear ?

EVE (*looking at* JUDY). I'd like everybody to get out of this room.

MR. JESSUP. Of course. Judy, run along, and don't worry your cousin. (*He bumps into* MRS. JESSUP.) I must finish shaving before this man arrives.

(HIGGINSON *enters from the door* L.)

HIGGINSON. Sir John Brent.

(JUDY *whistles.* MR. JESSUP *looks at her.*)

MR. JESSUP. Sir John who ?

HIGGINSON. Sir John Brent.

MR. JESSUP. Brent ?

HIGGINSON. That's what he says.

MR. JESSUP. But who is Sir John Brent ? And at this hour of the morning, too.

HIGGINSON. I don't know. I've put him in the drawing-room. (*With calm satisfaction.*) There's no fire.

(*Exit* HIGGINSON, L.)

(JUDY *whistles continuously, crossing to* C.)

MRS. JESSUP. And I'm still in my slippers.

(*Exit* MRS. JESSUP *into the bedroom up at back* L. *She shuts the bedroom door.*)

MR. JESSUP. And I'm not shaved. Sir John Brent. Now where have I heard that name before ? Stop *whistling*, Judy !

JUDY. He lives in the flat below, he moved in last week. You've seen his name on the board at the foot of the lift.

MR. JESSUP. But who is he ?

JUDY. He's a surgeon—a specialist—an ace. The hall porter told me. A hundred guineas per appendix, per person, per portion.

MR. JESSUP. I'm beginning to remember.

JUDY. They gave him a knighthood at the Coronation. They were rather dishing them out at the time. He's still quite good-looking. (*With intentional deliberation, glancing at* EVE.) Goggie and I came up in the lift with him the other day. He sort of squinted down his nose at us.

MR. JESSUP (*goes to the mirror—wipes his face. Desperately.*) But why *should* he come and pay a call on me, at this hour ?

JUDY. Because you have just invited him, darling !

MR. JESSUP. I ? What ? (*At the wash-basin.*)

JUDY. Yes, over the telephone, in a loud voice.

MR. JESSUP. Don't tell me he's Dr. Mackenzie's locum !

JUDY. I'm not going to.

(EVE *coughs.*)

MR. JESSUP. Then why is he here ?

JUDY. One of those wrong numbers, I suppose. Hadn't you better see him at once ?

(*Exit* MR. JESSUP, L.)

(JUDY *goes* L. *and examines the pad ;* EVE *jumps up hastily out of bed, crosses to the dressing-table and powders her nose ; then dips the thermometer afresh, in the teapot this time, and gets into bed.*)

(C.) And who wrote this number on this pad ? Full marks, darling ! (*She taps the pad.*) Very clever indeed ! But—I am surprised, you know. Our little Queen Sap, breaking out like this! Ah me! Youth, youth! (*She returns the pad* L.)

(EVE *burns her mouth with the thermometer*.)

(*Enter* MRS. JESSUP, L.)

MRS. JESSUP (*in a hurried whisper*). The doctor's here, Eve. Let me tidy that bed. (*She does so*.) He's not Dr. Mackenzie's locum at all. He's Sir John Brent, the great surgeon, But he says he'll see you. Of course, your father would muddle things. Here you are, Sir John. (*Shutting the bedroom door up* L.)

MR. JESSUP (*off stage*). This way, Sir John.

(*Enter* SIR JOHN BRENT—*a distinguished-looking man of thirty-seven, followed by* MR. JESSUP, *who has now got his face clean*.)

SIR JOHN (L. *of the bed. Advancing to* EVE's *bed and smiling at her*). And is this the patient?

MR. JESSUP. Our daughter, Eve. This is her little cousin, Judy.

(SIR JOHN *bows with exaggerated formality to* JUDY, *who giggles*.)

SIR JOHN. Good morning, ladies. (*To* JUDY.) I think we shared a lift the other morning. (*Then he turns to* EVE, *gravely*.) Miss Jessup, aren't you rather a bold young woman?

(EVE *looks startled*.)

I only saw people's arms and legs off : I haven't done any real medical work for about five years. Will you risk it ?

(EVE, *relieved, nods vigorously*.)

MR. JESSUP (*crosses to* C.). I'm sure it's very good of you to come at all, Sir John.

SIR JOHN. Well, of course, in the ordinary way this would be a serious breach of professional etiquette. But in an emergency, it's a case of the nearest man, isn't it ? (*Laying his hand on* EVE's *forehead, then taking the thermometer from her mouth*.) I can relieve your mind on one point, Mr. Jessup. Your daughter's life is in no immediate danger. (*Down* C., *followed by* JUDY.)

MR. JESSUP. You're quite sure ? (*He moves* JUDY *to* L.)

SIR JOHN. Positive. (*He crosses* R. *to the dressing-table*.)

MR. JESSUP (*fervently*. C.). Thank heaven for that !

MRS. JESSUP (L.). Aubrey, you'll be late for the office.

MR. JESSUP. Bless my soul, so I will, and I'm not dressed. Good-bye, Sir John ; good-bye, my pet (*he kisses* EVE) ; good-bye, Bertha !

(*He goes up, then down* L. *of* MRS. JESSUP, *and furtively hands a five-pound note to her, nods meaningly towards* SIR JOHN, *and hurries out* L.)

MRS. JESSUP (L. *of the bed—pushing* JUDY). What is her temperature, Sir John ?

SIR JOHN (R. *of the bed*).   It appears to be about a hundred and ten.

MRS. JESSUP.   There must be something wrong with the thermometer.

SIR JOHN.   It is doing its best.   A hundred and ten is as high as it can go.

EVE.   Please go away, Mummy, and take Judy with you.

(MRS. JESSUP *is about to refuse, but* SIR JOHN *nods to her.*)

SIR JOHN.   Patients sometimes describe their symptoms more readily without an audience.

MRS. JESSUP.   Well, just as you say, Sir John.   Don't hang about, child !

(*She hustles* JUDY L., *who is under her feet as usual, out of the room.*)

JUDY (*as she goes*).   Good-bye, Goggie !

(EVE *and* SIR JOHN *are now left alone.*)

SIR JOHN.   And why did your cousin address you as Goggie ?

EVE.   It's short for Goggle-Eyes.   (*Modestly.*)   I'm supposed to have rather big eyes.   (*Hiding the knickers from the chair* L. *under the pillow, as* SIR JOHN *crosses* L. *and puts the thermometer in the glass on the basin.*)

SIR JOHN.   The fact appears to me to be beyond the region of supposition.   H'm !   That reminds me, we must be regular about this.   (*He produces a memorandum book and pencil.*)   Your full name, please.   (*He sits on the chair* L. *of the bed.*)

EVE.   Eve Angela Bingley Jessup.

SIR JOHN.   What is the Bingley doing there ?

EVE.   Mother's maiden name.   That was why she married.

SIR JOHN.   (*Writing.*)   Age ?

EVE.   Eighteen.   That must seem horribly young to you.

SIR JOHN.   Why ?   (*Feeling her pulse.*)

EVE.   Well, you must be a lot more than that yourself.

SIR JOHN.   I'm thirty-seven.   I suppose that seems very old to you.

EVE.   Oh, no.   For a man—one simply couldn't bear to think of it !   I mean—*could* one ?

SIR JOHN.   I wonder if *you'll* say that when you are thirty-seven ?   H'm !   Pulse normal.   (*He puts his hand to her forehead.*)   Your high temperature appears to have subsided.   Will you tell me how that thermometer managed to register a hundred and ten degrees Fahrenheit ?

EVE.   I put it in the teapot !

(*They both laugh.*)

SIR JOHN (*rises*).   Eve Angela Bingley Jessup, I've done with you.

EVE (*kneeling*).   No—Sir John—please don't go yet.   I really *am* ill.

SIR JOHN.   How ill ?   And where ?

EVE.   I'm not certain ; but I read somewhere the other day that ninety per cent of people are ill without knowing it.

SIR JOHN.   You appear to be one of the more fortunate ten per cent.

EVE.   But one can't be sure.   I should like to be examined, please—from top to—— (*Hurriedly.*)   Will you examine me, please ?

(*She turns down the bedclothes and lies on her face, with her nose buried in the pillow.   SIR JOHN stands looking down on her.   He lifts his hand, as if to give her the good smack she deserves ; then drops it and smiles.*)

SIR JOHN.   The other way up, please.   (*She rolls over on her back, and he replaces the bedclothes.*)   Tongue !

(*EVE shows her tongue.*)

—Thank you ; that will be far enough.   Spoon.

(*She hands him the teaspoon from the tray.*)

—Open, please.   Ah !

(*EVE opens her mouth.   He holds down her tongue with the handle of the spoon, and examines her throat.*)

EVE (*gurgling*).   You're choking me.

SIR JOHN.   You deserve it.   (*He removes the spoon.*)

(*EVE takes it.*)

—Throat and tonsils entirely free from inflammation.   (*He feels her throat glands.*)   Does that hurt ?

EVE.   No.

SIR JOHN.   I'm sorry.

(*He puts his ear to her back and listens.*)

EVE.   Ninety-nine !

SIR JOHN.   I beg your pardon ?

EVE (*meekly*).   I thought I had to say that.

SIR JOHN.   Are you sure you didn't mean a hundred and ten ? (*Restoring her to a lying position.*)   Heart a little rapid, but strong and regular.   Nothing wrong there.

EVE.   Oh, but there is !

SIR JOHN.   Are you trying to teach me my business ?

EVE (*kneels up again*).   Oh no, no, *no* !   But what I mean is, your heart sometimes—your heart sometimes makes you do things you hadn't meant to do at all. (*Hesitating.*) Especially when—when——

Sir John. Especially when it's the first real day of spring, and you can't bear the idea of going and sitting in a stuffy class-room ! When you want to run wild across green grass, with the wind in your face. Let off steam—shout—dance—because it's April, and you're young !

Eve (*nodding*). Yes—yes ! Did you want to do that too, when you were young ? (*Politely.*) Ages ago, of course.

Sir John. Perhaps I did. Not so many ages ago, either. Well, we have now diagnosed your complaint. An aggravated attack of—shall we say ?—truantitis !

Eve. Truant——? (*She laughs, nodding.*) I see. Did you make that name up ?

Sir John. This very moment.

Eve. For me ?

Sir John. For you.

Eve (*sitting up*). I've had a disease named after me ! Tell me all about it. Is it dangerous ?

Sir John. No ; but it's highly infectious.

Eve. Have you caught it ?

(*He nods, moving back a pace.*)

From me ?

(*He nods again and smiles.*)

—Lovely ! (*She claps her hands.*)

Sir John. Lovely ? It's most unprofessional. I don't know what I'm thinking of. I *must* go. I'm surprised at you. I'm surprised at myself. Good morning ! (*He puts out his hand to say good-bye.*)

Eve (*seizing his hand*). Just two minutes more ! There's something I want to ask you. I want to ask you how you understood so well about wanting to run and shout. Across the grass—wind in your face—and all that !

Sir John. Perhaps because I've had so few chances to do such things myself. (*He crosses to the wash-basin up* L. *to wash his hands*). I worked very hard when I was young. The industrious apprentice, you know. But not of my own free will—oh no ! I was poor, desperately poor. I had to support myself by doing odd jobs all the time I was qualifying.

Eve. What did you do ?

Sir John. A little tutoring one term. I helped a chemist to make up prescriptions another. Oh, yes, and once I took over an envelope-addressing job.

Eve. No !

Sir John. That was the worst.

Eve. Did you have to lick the envelopes, too ?

SIR JOHN. Yes, and the stamps.

EVE. Did you swallow *all* the gum ?

SIR JOHN. No,—after the first thousand envelopes, I could chew it. (*He comes back to* C., *wiping his hands.*) Anyhow, I could never afford to join clubs or play games, or have any sort of recreations.

EVE. What a shame ! But you can afford to play now.

SIR JOHN. Yes, I suppose I can. But I don't—perhaps because I never learned how. I seem to enjoy work better. Work is rather absorbing, you know. It gets possession after a while.

EVE. What exactly do you do ? Please tell me. (*She kneels on the bed.*)

SIR JOHN (*puts the towel back on the basin up* L.). Well, this morning I have a couple of operations waiting for me at a nursing-home in Bentinck Street. After that I shall go round a surgical ward in St. Barnabas' Hospital, followed by a mob of students, and tell them, in a confident voice, a lot of things that I'm not sure of, and which they won't believe. This afternoon I shall spend from four till six in my consulting-room, seeing patients.

EVE. Women ?

SIR JOHN. Mostly.

EVE. Attractive ?

SIR JOHN. A doctor never notices a patient's looks !

EVE. What, never ?

SIR JOHN. Well, hardly ever.

(*Looking hard at her. They both laugh.*)

—After dinner I am lecturing to a very dull society on a disease which you never even heard of, and I hope never will.

EVE (*rapturously*). Now I shall be able to follow you all day. But you don't lecture every evening ?

SIR JOHN. Oh, no.

EVE. Don't you go to parties, ever ?

SIR JOHN (*crosses to the bed*). Yes, sometimes, but they're no fun. Not by oneself, anyhow. Shall I tell you a pet belief of mine ?

EVE (*thrilled at being taken into his confidence*). Please.

SIR JOHN. Here's a question. What makes every human experience worth while ?

EVE. Why, having it !

SIR JOHN. That's rather a lovely answer—the answer of youth. But you're wrong. (*He brings a chair down to the bed and sits.*) Not having it—sharing it !

EVE. Sharing it ?

SIR JOHN. Yes, that's what matters. An adventure is no fun if you have it all by yourself, or if there isn't someone you can tell about it afterwards. That's the important bit—being

B

able to tell someone about things afterwards : it makes the pleasant things enjoyable and the unpleasant ones endurable. Whichever they were, you can laugh over them—together.

Eve. I see. And haven't you anybody to tell about things ?

Sir John. No.

Eve. That must be pretty awful sometimes. Of course, I can always tell Judy.

Sir John. That's the young lady with the decided manner ?

Eve. Yes. She calls for me every morning, and we go to school together.

Sir John. Where ?

Eve. St. Anselm's, in Baywater—a big day school Have you heard of it ?

Sir John. Yes. A most select establishment, I gather.

Eve. Horribly. Judy nearly got expelled the other day. The next time she'll go. And if she does, Uncle Ken has threatened to send her to a place in Regent's Park that's practically a reformatory. Its called the Euphemia Tadworthy Foundation.

Sir John (*smiling*). There is no danger of that happening to you, I hope ?

Eve. Oh no, I don't think so. It's a funny thing, but nothing ever seems to happen to me at school. I like work. I don't know why.

Sir John (*rising ; sternly*). Then why are you lying in that bed to-day—malingering ?

Eve. You've just told me yourself. Truantitis—spring—grass—trees—— (*She is conscious of his stern gaze, and tails off with a gulp.*)

Sir John. No other reason ?

(*She shakes her head.*)

—Cross your heart ?

(*She nods vigorously. He shakes his head. He groans.*)

Eve. Why are you doing that ? (*She puts the chair up stage.*)

Sir John. Remorse. You're a fraud, and so am I. You're shamming, and I'm abetting you. It's time I went and cut off somebody's leg. (*He offers his hand.*) Good-bye.

(*He hesitates. She looks up at him, very wide-eyed indeed.*)

Eve. I'm glad Daddy got that wrong number.

Sir John. Are you quite sure it was a wrong number ?

(*He reads the truth in her eyes, and turns her head sharply up towards him.*)

Eve. What are you trying to do ?

Sir John. I'm about to wring your little neck.

(*Enter* Mrs. Jessup, l. *He drops her head rather hastily.*)

(*Professionally.*) No, your head is quite cool again, Miss Eve.
(*He turns to* MRS. JESSUP.)

MRS. JESSUP. Is it anything serious, Sir John ?

SIR JOHN. Oh dear, no. A trifling ailment of youth, especially common at this time of year.

MRS. JESSUP. Not infectious, of course ?

SIR JOHN. Of course not !

(EVE *gives a sudden chuckle, and rolls over, burying her face in the
pillow. He turns quickly and glares at her, then offers his hand
to* MRS. JESSUP.)

Good-bye ! (*To* MRS. JESSUP.)

MRS. JESSUP (L.C., *nervously proffering the five-pound note*).
Will you—I mean—as a specialist, I suppose you would prefer
——

SIR JOHN. Leave it for the moment, please. I shall be
coming to see my patient again to-morrow. (*He crosses down* L.)

MRS. JESSUP. Oh, but how very kind !

(*They disappear* R., *talking :* " And the treatment ? " " I'll
attend to that." *Etc.*)

> *The moment they are gone,* EVE *leaps out of bed, runs to the
> door, and looks out after them. She kisses her hand, then runs
> back to her bed and jumps up and down.*
> JUDY *enters. She takes a look at* EVE ; *then walks to the
> dressing-table, picks up the bottle of scent, puts on the scarf as a
> veil, and goes out, singing " The Wedding March."*

QUICK CURTAIN.

SCENE 2

SCENE.—*The hall of* SIR JOHN BRENT'S *house in Bryanston Square.
Almost any good interior set will serve for this room, but three
doors are essential—one* L., *leading to the front door, one* R.,
*leading into the consulting-room direct, and one fairly large
opening at the back, showing a passage or inner hall. It is
assumed that the pantry is off* R. *from this, and the drawing-room
and staircase off* L.
Essential furniture :* C. *a settee, facing straight down stage,
with a refectory table close behind it. Up at the back, a sideboard
or bureau. A chair* R. *of the table. A mirror hanging on the
wall* R. *Under the mirror a table, with a telephone.*

(*Voices are heard off* R., *saying good-bye.*)

SIR JOHN. Good-bye, Sir Theodore. Good-bye.

SIR THEODORE. Give our kindest regards to your little wife.

(SIR JOHN *enters.*)

SIR JOHN. Thank you. (*Turning.*) She'll be terribly disappointed at missing you. (*He shuts the door.*)

(MRS. JESSUP *enters up stage.* SIR JOHN *fills a pipe at the table* R.)

(*Below the table to* R.) Well, that's the last of the sherry party. (R.C.)

MRS. JESSUP (*behind the table*). A sherry party without a hostess ! What time is it ?

SIR JOHN. Getting on for seven.

MRS. JESSUP. And she isn't in yet. Where is she ?

SIR JOHN (*solemnly*). I haven't the slightest idea.

MRS. JESSUP (*moves to him*). But you ought to have. And you ought to be angry with her.

SIR JOHN. Nobody could be angry with her.

MRS. JESSUP. Couldn't they ? You wait !

(*Enter* MR. JESSUP L.)

MR. JESSUP (*fussily ;* L. *of the table* C.). Something must have happened to the child. Do you think we should ring up all the hospitals ? (L.C.)

MRS. JESSUP. It would be quicker to ring up all the cinemas. She's probably wandered into one and fallen into a trance over Fred Astaire. (*She crosses to the settee.*)

MR. JESSUP. Bertha, don't be heartless.

MRS. JESSUP (*sits* R. *end of the settee*). And don't be a fussy breeches, Aubrey. Go and see if the car is there.

(MR. JESSUP *hurries into the vestibule.*)

All the same, I would like to know where she is.

SIR JOHN. Eve will turn up. Punctuality's not one of her noticeable virtues.

MRS. JESSUP. You talk as if she possessed all the others.

SIR JOHN. Well, doesn't she ?

MRS. JESSUP. No.

SIR JOHN. My dear mother-in-law, allow me to know something about my own wife.

MRS. JESSUP (*grimly*). When you've been married to her longer than six weeks, you'll begin to know a good deal more. She's as unscrupulous as Judy really, only not quite so blatantly crude in her methods.

SIR JOHN (*chuckling*). Judy ! By the way, I like Judy's mother. (R.C.)

MRS. JESSUP. Cynthia ? Yes, poor woman, so do I. It's wonderful how she manages to keep up her spirits. (R. *of the couch.*)

SIR JOHN. Why ?

MRS. JESSUP. She is married to my brother. You haven't seen very much of him yet, have you ?

SIR JOHN. No.

MRS. JESSUP. When you do, avoid all reference to internal organs.

SIR JOHN. Thanks, I will. By the way, why did Judy get sacked from St. Anselm's ?

MRS. JESSUP. Cynthia wouldn't tell me. I'll get it out of Kenneth sooner or later.

(*Enter* GRAVES *from* L., *and announces* MRS. BINGLEY.)

GRAVES (*at the door* L.). Mrs. Bingley.

(*Exit* GRAVES L., *and shuts the door.*)

(MRS. BINGLEY, JUDY'S *mother, enters* L. *She is clutching a bottle of milk of magnesia. She is a pleasant, humorous, talkative but tactful woman of about thirty-five.*)

MRS. JESSUP. Cynthia ! (L. *of the table* C.)

MRS. BINGLEY. Yes, here I am, darlings.

(SIR JOHN *goes to meet her. They shake hands.*)

So sorry to be late, but we've been interviewing the headmistress of Tadworthy Lodge.

SIR JOHN (*above the table*). What is she like ?

MRS. BINGLEY (*sits on the settee*, L. *end*). Hitler, only a better moustache. My old man and Judy are still there. She was reading aloud to them when I left.

MRS. JESSUP. What ?

MRS. BINGLEY. It sounded like the Thirty-Nine Articles, only there were more of them. She gave me a copy for myself. Would you like it, John ? (*She hands the pamphlet to* SIR JOHN.)

SIR JOHN. Thank you. (*Indicating the bottle.*) Did she give you that, too ?

MRS. BINGLEY. No, I bought that on my way here—for Ken. Milk of magnesia. Curried prawns at lunch—he would ! (*She puts the bottle on the table.*)

SIR JOHN (*reading*). The Tadworthy Constitution.

MRS. BINGLEY. Penned by that remarkable woman Euphemia Tadworthy herself.

MRS. JESSUP. How do you know ?

MRS. BINGLEY. Miss Philpott told me—the headmistress.

SIR JOHN (*examining the pamphlet*). Euphemia seems to have been a lady of decided views. (*He reads.*) Listen to this. Article 4. " School bills shall be presented, not to parent or guardian, but to the pupil herself. They shall be checked by the pupil herself, and paid by the pupil herself."

MRS. JESSUP. Why ?

MRS. BINGLEY (*pointing*). To correct early fixations, and inculcate self-reliance.

SIR JOHN. Ah ! Here's a good one. " Reports on conduct." This will shake Judy up. " Reports on conduct, whether favourable or adverse, are handed to the pupil instead of being sent home." " Are handed to the pupil "—that lets Judy out, doesn't it ?

MRS. BINGLEY. Read on.

SIR JOHN. " The Pupil, however, is required to produce documentary evidence that she has shown these to her parents." I have a feeling that Judy isn't going to enjoy this place much. What do you think, Mr. Jessup ?

(*Enter* MR. JESSUP, L.)

MR. JESSUP. I am thinking of one thing only at this moment —what has become of my daughter ?

MRS. BINGLEY. Yes—what has become of her ? Where's the sherry party that I was invited to ?

MRS. JESSUP. The sherry party has broken up.

MRS. BINGLEY. So early ? Where's Eve ?

MRS. JESSUP. Nobody knows.

SIR JOHN. She hasn't come in yet.

MR. JESSUP. Do you think she's been kidnapped ? What is the number of Scotland Yard ?

(*Exit* MR. JESSUP *into the consulting-troom,* R.)

SIR JOHN (*to* MRS. JESSUP). Stop him !

MRS. JESSUP. Trust me.

(*Exit* MRS. JESSUP *into the consulting-room,* R.)

MRS. BINGLEY. Are you worried, my dear ?

SIR JOHN. No, not really. The child has no sense of time, that's all. (*He sits on the settee,* R. *end.*)

MRS. BINGLEY. Has this happened before ?

SIR JOHN. Yes, last week I asked old Mellish and his Lady to tea to make her acquaintance. He's chairman of the hospital——

MRS. BINGLEY. And of course, important to you. Well, what happened ?

SIR JOHN. Nothing ! No Eve ! She was eventually run to earth in the mews, having tea with my chauffeur's children. She'd just forgotten. That's all. Bless her !

(*Enter* MR. *and* MRS. JESSUP, *from the consulting-room,* R.)

MR. JESSUP. Yes ! Bless her !

MRS. JESSUP. Bless her ! And that's all any of you can say !

SIR JOHN. It is. And always will be! Now come and see our drawing-room, Cynthia, and have that sherry.

(*They all make a move* L.)

(*Enter* HIGGINSON *from up* R.)

HIGGINSON (*calmly*). It's all right. She's home!

OMNES. Home!

SIR JOHN. How did she come in?

HIGGINSON. By the side door, two minutes ago.

MR. JESSUP. By the side door? I knew it! She was carried in! (*He crosses* L. *to* MRS. JESSUP.)

HIGGINSON. She was pushed in—by a couple of newspaper boys. Friends of hers, she said.

OMNES. Newspaper boys?

SIR JOHN. But where is she now?

HIGGINSON. Washing her face at the pantry sink. It needed it. (*Going up and looking off* R. *Calling to* EVE.) You can come in. The party's over!

EVE (*off stage*). Over . . .? Oh, lovely! (*She appears, hat in one hand and comb in the other, and a towel round her neck. She runs in and rushes to* SIR JOHN.) Say I'm forgiven, please. (*She kisses him.*) Please. I'll confess everything. Don't scold me, please. (*She embraces everyone in turn.*)

(SIR JOHN *takes the towel and the comb from her and hands them to* HIGGINSON, *who exits with them into the pantry.*)

MRS. JESSUP. Of course he won't scold you. He never does. (*To* SIR JOHN.) Why don't you lay her across your knee for once?

MR. JESSUP. Bertha! (*To* EVE.) What happened, darling? An accident?

EVE. I'm not sure. One man in the crowd bet another a thousand pounds that it had been done on purpose. He didn't look as if he *had* a thousand pounds.

MRS. JESSUP ⎫
MRS. BINGLEY ⎬ (*together*).
MR. JESSUP ⎭

⎧ What had been done on purpose?
⎨ What crowd, dear?
⎩ Why a thousand pounds?

EVE. Isn't it marvellous how crowds spring up in London? It was rather terrifying, all the same. I've never been close to a really big one before. The engines, and the hose, and the ladder, and——

MR. JESSUP. Great heavens! Have you been in a fire?

EVE. Well, not right in it, Daddy. The police held us back. (*She pushes them all back.*) They were all across the street.

MRS. JESSUP. What street?

MRS. BINGLEY. Where was the fire?

EVE. I'm not sure, dear. We just followed the engines. I'd

never have got there if Alfie hadn't pulled me along for the last half-mile. He was an angel.

MR. JESSUP. Who is——?

MRS. JESSUP. How long did you stay there ?

EVE. What time is it now ?

MR. JESSUP. Nearly seven.

EVE. I'd no idea ! (*She crosses to* SIR JOHN R.) We had to wait for the roof to fall in. That's always the best part, Alfie said.

MR. JESSUP. Who is Alfie ?

EVE. A newspaper boy, darling.

(*Enter* GRAVES *from the consulting-room,* R. *and stands just inside the doorway.*)

MRS. JESSUP (C.). I am going home ! Aubrey !

GRAVES. There's a patient in the waiting-room, Sir John.

SIR JOHN. One moment !

(EVE *runs and kisses her father.*)

MR. JESSUP. Good-bye, darling. Please be less adventurous. (*He crosses down* L.)

MRS. JESSUP. Can I give you a lift, Cynthia ? (C.)

(EVE *turns and makes a face. Evidently she wants her to stay.*)

MRS. BINGLEY. No, thank you, dear. I want to hear more about the fire. (*She sits* L. *of the sofa.*) It sounds perfectly grand to me.

(EVE *crosses to the sofa and sits on the table behind.*)

SIR JOHN. Good-bye, and thank you both for coming. (*He shakes hands.*)

MRS. JESSUP. Not at all. (*Over at the door* L. *As she moves to go* L.) She is your responsibility now, thank Heaven !

EVE
MRS. BINGLEY } (*together*). Good-bye.

(*Exit* MR. *and* MRS. JESSUP L.)

(SIR JOHN *exits into the consulting-room* R. GRAVES *holds the door open for him and shuts it again.*)

EVE. Graves, will you ask them to send me up some tea, please—in a nice big kitchen cup ?

GRAVES. Very good, my lady.

(*Exit* GRAVES *up* R.)

MRS. BINGLEY. Well ? (*She sits* L. *of the settee,* EVE *on the refectory table, her feet on the settee.*)

EVE. Cynthia, I want to ask you something. What do young married women do in the daytime ?

MRS. BINGLEY. Get into mischief, most of them.

EVE. But I don't want to get into mischief.

MRS. BINGLEY. Bless my soul! Are you so much in love with Jack as all that?

EVE. I adore him!

MRS. BINGLEY. And yet when your hero comes home early to throw a sherry party for you—you're out!

EVE. I know, darling—and that just proves it.

MRS. BINGLEY. Proves what?

EVE. How lonely I am. I've so little to do that when there *is* something to do, I've thought of something else, so I'm not there to do the thing there *is* to do. Do you understand?

MRS. BINGLEY. Not a word—but I sympathize.

EVE. Bless you, angel. I mean, what hope have I? Jack's out of the house by dawn, practically, and I have to invent things to do until he comes home at night. It's a terribly long day to fill in.

MRS. BINGLEY. Proceed with the time-table. After breakfast, interview with cook?

EVE. Yes, and there's not the slightest need. She's been with Jack for years and knows exactly what he likes. If I contradicted her, she'd take me by the pants and run me out of the kitchen.

MRS. BINGLEY. What do you do next?

EVE. I go to the movies a good lot.

MRS. BINGLEY. At ten o'clock in the morning?

EVE (*sadly*). They don't open any earlier.

MRS. BINGLEY. Merciful heavens! But can't you cultivate some other amusement? Take riding lessons?

EVE. I can ride already.

MRS. BINGLEY. Bridge?

EVE. I talk all the time.

MRS. BINGLEY. Well, dressmakers! Fittings! You have a dress allowance?

EVE. Yes. (*She rises, goes up to the desk to get a photo out of the drawers.*) Yes, and do you know where I should like to get my clothes?

MRS. BINGLEY. I tremble to think.

EVE. I'll show you. (*She hands a framed photo of herself in gymnasium costume from the bureau.*) Like that.

MRS. BINGLEY. But, my child, you look quite nice in these. (*She hands back the photo.*)

EVE. I know. (*She puts back the photo.*) I've got a schoolgirl figure, I suppose.

MRS. BINGLEY. You're a schoolgirl from every angle. Yes, angle's the word. Look at you!

EVE. I know: it's pathetic.

Mrs. Bingley. I wouldn't worry. Time, the great healer, my dear.

(Graves *enters up* R. *with* Eve's *tea.*)

Graves. Your tea, my lady.
Eve. Thank you, Graves.

(Graves *puts down the tea on* R. *of the table and goes into the drawing-room, up* L.)

But I look so much younger than Jack ; younger even than I really am. When I'm fifty he'll be sixty-nine—if he's alive, of course, and I'm not a widow——
Mrs. Bingley. And when you're a hundred he'll be a hundred and nineteen. It's too awful to contemplate.

(Eve *brings tea to* Mrs. Bingley *and sits.*)

Don't fidget, and listen ! My precious, between a man and woman age doesn't matter one little bit. Take me and my old misery for instance.
Eve. Uncle Ken ?
Mrs. Bingley. The same. When I first met him I was a poor little shrimp like you—and he was a Cavalry Colonel, full vintage, with a D.S.O. and lady-friends and everything. I was married to him from school, thrilled to the bone and scared stiff. And in six months I had him—well——
Eve. Eating out of your hand.
Mrs. Bingley. No ; that was just the one thing he didn't do. If he had, I wouldn't have had to buy that for him to-day. (*She indicates the milk of magnesia.*) So start in at once. The first thing a husband has to be taught is just where he gets off in his own house. Does John try to boss you at all ?
Eve. Oh no, no, no ! He just spoils me—but he never makes a real companion of me. He never talks to me about his work—and heaven knows he has enough of it, poor lamb !
Mrs. Bingley. My dear, the whole world is divided between people with too much to do and people with too little. Never be sorry for the people with too much, because they're the only really happy ones.
Eve. I know all about the ones with too little, anyhow.
Mrs. Bingley. Besides, all these moans about overwork are just a bit of male propaganda. Still, John must learn to take you more seriously. We must think of something.

(*A loud door-knocker off* L.)

(Graves *enters up* L. *and goes out to the front door.*)

Eve (*is* R. *of the table*). Another patient, Graves ?

(*The door-knocker is banged several times.*)

GRAVES. It doesn't sound like a patient to me, madam.

MRS. BINGLEY. If it is, it's somebody who's been postponing his decease till the eleventh hour.

(The door is heard opening L.)

JUDY'S VOICE. Hallo, Graves, my pet!

(She enters, dressed in the Tadworthy uniform, which is a gymnasium suit of scarlet, with a scarlet cloak and beret and black stockings. She is carrying a small suitcase which she puts L. *end of the table.)*

JUDY. Hallo, Goggie!

(Enter COLONEL BINGLEY, L. *He is a stout, stolid man with a fixed expression and a gruff manner.)*

(She puts down the suitcase in front of the table.) Anybody want a hearty guffaw? *(She shows her clothes.)*

*(*GRAVES *goes to the pantry.)*

COLONEL *(gloomily)*. That's what she wears, from now on. Everything but horns and a tail. *(He moves behind the table to* R.C.)

EVE (R.C.). Poor Judy! *(Kissing* COLONEL BINGLEY.) How nice of you to come, Uncle Ken. How are you?

COLONEL. If I were to tell you, you wouldn't believe me. Nobody would. Where's your husband?

EVE. In the consulting-room.

COLONEL. Good! *(He goes* R.)

MRS. BINGLEY. With a patient.

COLONEL. I can wait. What's another five minutes, after years of it? *(He sits* R. *end of the table.)*

EVE. Have some sherry, Uncle Ken?

COLONEL. Sherry? Me? Suicide! Try Cynthia.

MRS. BINGLEY. Oh, thank you, dear. Where?

EVE. This way. *(She moves up* R.)

COLONEL. I'm waiting here for John.

(Exit EVE, JUDY, MRS. BINGLEY, *into the dining-room, up* R.)

(Enter SIR JOHN *from the consulting-room,* R.)

SIR JOHN *(seeing* COLONEL). Oh, hullo!

COLONEL. Oh, John! May I call you John?

SIR JOHN. Certainly, Kenneth.

COLONEL. Can I consult you in there for a few minutes, old chap? Just in the family way, of course.

SIR JOHN. *What?*

COLONEL. Between relations. Semi-professional.

SIR JOHN. I get you. What's the trouble?

COLONEL. Old man liver—with complications. I thought it

might amuse you to give me the once-over. It always seems to amuse my regular feller. He told me yesterday that life wouldn't seem the same when I was gone.

SIR JOHN. How much longer does he expect you to last ?

COLONEL. Oh, we're only going to Aix ! We're off to-morrow. We'd have gone sooner, only we had to get that little devil Judy arranged for. She's to board there while we're away ; and if she gets sacked again I've told her I'll skin her alive.

SIR JOHN. What was she sacked for last time ?

COLONEL. Forgery. Took a day off from school, and then put my name to a chit saying she'd been in bed with influenza. She'd have got away with it, too, if she hadn't spelt influenza with an " r " !

SIR JOHN. Come on. (*Going* R.)

COLONEL. I'm not exactly a teetotaller——

(*They both exit* R.)

(JUDY *appears with* EVE *up* R.)

JUDY. Well, if I can't have sherry, can I have some tea ?

EVE. I'll ring for another cup.

JUDY. This saucer will do. (*She sits* L. *of the table, pours tea into the saucer and drinks it.*)

EVE (*looking at the suitcase*). What's this ?

JUDY. The Tadworthy holdall. Open it.

(EVE *kneels and does so, and takes things out.*)

—Sabbath attire. Gymnasium ditto. Emergency bloomers. (*She drinks tea out of the saucer.*) Essential books, including

(EVE *lays books on the table.*)

—Hall and Knight's " Algebra "—I should like to burn Hall and boil Knight—and the " Oxford Book of English Verse "—most of the latter to be committed to memory, I fear.

EVE (*examining the books eagerly*). What a lot of fun !

JUDY. And she means it ! Let me sell you these—and you can read them when Jack's out. Half a minute. (*She examines the insides of the book-covers.*) One pound I'm asking. (*Offering the books.*) One quid—fifteen bob—ten—five—half-a-crown for the lot !

EVE. But what will you do without them ?

JUDY (*puts books back in the case*). Get a second-hand set, and thereby reap a modest profit. There are people with suites at Claridge's to-day who started that way. No ?

EVE. No.

JUDY. Well, I leave the offer open. What about giving this new domicile of yours the once-over ? Is it nice upstairs ? Is the nuptial chamber luxurious ?

EVE. Come up, and I'll show you.

JUDY. I'll race you. Get to your marks.

(*They go up.*)

Are you ready ? Off !

(JUDY *dashes off up* L. *upstairs and disappears.* EVE *about to follow.*)

(MRS. BINGLEY *has appeared from the drawing-room.*)

MRS. BINGLEY. Eve !

EVE (*coming back*). Yes, dear ?

MRS. BINGLEY. Have you got a smart evening frock—something out of your trousseau that you've never worn before ?

EVE. Yes—one I'm a little bit shy about wearing. No sleeves—no back——

MRS. BINGLEY. That's the one. How long will it take you to put it on ?

EVE. Three minutes.

MRS. BINGLEY. Well, go and do it.

EVE. Why, darling ? Is there going to be——?

MRS. BINGLEY. Don't ask questions ! (*She gives* EVE *a friendly smack.*) Up you go !

EVE. All right ! (*She runs off up* L.)

(MRS. BINGLEY *goes to the consulting-room door. She knocks, then steps back.*)

MRS. BINGLEY. John !

(SIR JOHN *appears at the door.*)

I want to talk to you—and not about my inside. Send Ken away.

COLONEL'S VOICE. He can't. I've got my shirt off, damn it !

MRS. BINGLEY. Very well ; stay there. (*She crosses him and closes the door.*)

SIR JOHN. And what can I do for you, madam ?

MRS. BINGLEY. Have you anything on to-night—engagement of any kind ?

SIR JOHN (*suspiciously*). Woman, what do you want me to do ?

MRS. BINGLEY. I want you to take your wife out.

SIR JOHN. We're dining at home, and then I have a thesis to write.

MRS. BINGLEY. You're dining at the Savoy Grill. Something quite light, because it will be early. Then you are going to a thoroughly frivolous play. After that you will take supper at the Berkeley. Can people get tight there ?

Sir John. I shouldn't think it was encouraged.

Mrs. Bingley. Well, ask the head waiter. If he says no, go somewhere else, and *get* tight. Not audibly or visibly, but just enough to thaw you into some semblance of a human being. That's all, I think. Go and tell her. Remember, this is all your idea, and not mine.

Sir John. Getting tight ?

Mrs. Bingley. The party, imbecile !

Sir John. But I tell you I've got some work to do.

Mrs. Bingley. You certainly have. You've got to make a fuss of her from now on.

Sir John. I'm not demonstrative by nature, you know.

Mrs. Bingley. That's why you've to get tight, silly. Now listen : as soon as you reach the articulate stage, which should be in about half a bottle, ask her if she is happy. She will reply, yes, of course. You will then call her a little liar, and ask what you can do to make her really happy.

Sir John. All that on half a bottle ? Why ?

Mrs. Bingley. Because the child is desperately lonely and bored stiff, (*shouting*) and it's all your fault !

(Graves *enters up* R., *with a butler's tray—spoons, forks, etc.*)

(*Pushing* Sir John *aside she crosses* R.C.) Take that away ! Sir John and her Ladyship are dining out. (*To* Sir John.) Aren't you ? Yes !

(Graves *goes out, bewildered.*)

(Mrs. Bingley *opens the door of the consulting-room and calls.*)

You there—got your shirt on yet ?

Colonel's Voice. It's on, but not in.

Mrs. Bingley. Hurry up, and come home ! (*She crosses to behind the table.*)

Colonel (*appearing at the door*). But I'm consulting John.

Mrs. Bingley. Yes ; and a fat lot of advice he'll give you for what you're thinking of paying ! You'll do better on milk—— (*She takes the bottle.*)

Colonel. Milk ? (*He crosses to* C. *in front of the settee.*)

Mrs. Bingley. Of magnesia. Get your hat.

Colonel. Where's that brat Judy ?

Mrs. Bingley. Upstairs with Eve. Send her home when she comes down, John. Au revoir ! You can report progress to me in about a fortnight's time.

Colonel. Whose progress ?

Mrs. Bingley. Eve's. (*She crosses to him.*)

Colonel (*interested*). What—Eve ? Already ?

MRS. BINGLEY. Out!

(*She hustles him out. The front door bangs.*)

(SIR JOHN *stands thinking; then goes up and calls off up* L.)

SIR JOHN. Eve!

EVE'S VOICE. Yes, darling?

SIR JOHN. Come here a moment, will you? And don't slide down the banisters!

EVE'S VOICE. I can't.

(*She appears from up* L., *looking radiant, in a shimmering evening frock.* SIR JOHN *is struck dumb.*)

What's the matter? Don't you like me? Is it a bit too—you know?

SIR JOHN (*he puts his arm round her*). Darling, shall I tell you something—confess something?

EVE. Yes, please.

SIR JOHN. Ever since I married you I've felt a bit of a cradle-robber—a baby-snatcher. Now I don't, any more! In that frock you're a woman—for the first time. It's given me an inspiration. To-night you and I are going out on a bender together.

EVE. No. We're dining at home. Cook told me.

SIR JOHN. Dinner has been cancelled.

EVE. By you?

SIR JOHN. Most certainly by me! You're coming to the Savoy Grill. Then we'll go to a play. Then supper——

EVE (*turns and leans against him excitedly*). Oh, darling—bless you! Why?

SIR JOHN. Because I want to see if we can't recapture a little honeymoon atmosphere. Could that be done, do you think?

EVE. Good gracious, yes! Shut your eyes?

(*Both shut their eyes.*)

Where are we? Paris—Buda Pesth—Venice?

SIR JOHN. Venice.

EVE. Right. Can you see the Grand Canal?

SIR JOHN. No, but I can smell it.

(EVE *opens her eyes and gives him a little slap.*)

EVE. That ruins it. Try again. The Grand Canal. We're in a gondola.

SIR JOHN. In a gondola?

EVE. By moonlight.

SIR JOHN. By moonlight.

EVE. Do you remember our first gondola by moonlight?

SIR JOHN. Distinctly.

EVE. And what the gondolier said ?

SIR JOHN. Vividly.

EVE. Rather familiar, I thought.

SIR JOHN. That's what he said *we* were ! Oh, I didn't mind *him*. The man I did *not* like was the hotel clerk at Buda Pesth, who said he supposed my daughter would like a room fairly near mine ! Daughter !

EVE. He wouldn't have said that a week or two later. By the time we came home I had got you down to about twenty-eight.

SIR JOHN. To-night I feel about twenty-four—— Well, a youngish twenty-five.

EVE. Sure ?

SIR JOHN. Positive !

EVE. Then race me upstairs. I can beat Judy at it. I'll have three yards start. Wait till I pick up this skirt of mine. Are you ready ? One, two, three, go !

(*They start off up* L *; she trips. He picks her up and helps her to the sofa.*)

SIR JOHN. Are you hurt, darling ?

EVE. I think I've broken something.

SIR JOHN. Good gracious, what ?

EVE. A suspender.

(*Telephone.*)

(GRAVES *enters up* R. *and answers.*)

GRAVES. The hospital, Sir John. Urgent.

(SIR JOHN *takes the receiver.*)

(GRAVES *exit.*)

SIR JOHN. Yes, John Brent speaking. The hospital—yes ? Who wants me ? Very well, put me through to him—— Hallo, is that you, Walter ? What's the trouble ? To-night ! Immediately ! Well, can't the House Surgeon—— The fact is, I've just arranged—— Where's Sir James ? Very well, old man, I'll be along in twenty minutes. Tell Sister to get things ready. Good-bye.

(EVE *has been listening. We see her face and attitude as she realizes that her evening out is cancelled.* SIR JOHN *goes into the consulting-room* R., *and returns with a small despatch-case.*)

I'm sorry, my sweet ; the party's off.

EVE. Off—altogether ?

SIR JOHN. For to-night, anyhow. You see, I've got to operate right away : there's nobody else for the moment. It's a case we've been observing very carefully for two or three days—

waiting for something to mature. (*He takes a note-book from the case, consults it, and puts it back.*) And now it's happened before its time. I'm afraid you'll have to dine at home to-night, after all. I'm so sorry.

(SIR JOHN *rings the bell* L., *and crosses to* L. *of the table.*)

EVE. No, you're not. You're not sorry one little bit. You're rather relieved. You've got out of something you didn't want to do. You're going to do a nice messy operation instead. And now you are happy !

SIR JOHN (L. *of the table*). Don't talk nonsense, dear. Why do you think I suggested going out ?

EVE (*to* R. *of the table*). I don't know. Yes, I do ! Cynthia ! she put you up to it. Didn't she ?

SIR JOHN. Guilty ! I ought to have thought of it myself ! I'm sorry again.

(*Enter* GRAVES *from the pantry, comes behind the table* C.)

EVE. That telephone call was a godsend to you—or did you arrange it ?

SIR JOHN. My dear, you're behaving like a child.

(*She turns her back.*)

Graves, I have to go to the hospital at once. (*He gives* GRAVES *the despatch-case.*) Her Ladyship will dine at home after all.

GRAVES. Shall I ring for the car, Sir John ?

SIR JOHN. There's no time ; I'll take a taxi.

(GRAVES *crosses to the door* L.)

You can send the car to the hospital about eleven.

(*Exit* GRAVES L.)

Good night, Eve. (*He goes to her and kisses the back of her neck. Then crosses to the door* L.)

EVE. Is it a woman or a man you are operating on ?

SIR JOHN (*crossing to the door* L. *At the door*). A woman. She is seventy-two. Good night !

(*Exit* SIR JOHN.)

(GRAVES *re-enters, takes the teatray, and crosses to the pantry* R. *and exit.*)

(EVE *controls herself until he is gone, then turns her head away, sobbing.*)

(*Enter* JUDY, *whistling,* L.)

JUDY. I like your house dear. H. & C., central heating, modern sanitation. (*She turns.*) Hallo, what's the matter ? Blubbing ?

EVE. No.

JUDY. Yes, you are.

EVE. All right—I am. (*She sits* L. *of the settee.*)

JUDY. Very well, then. I suppose you're not going to tell me why ?

EVE. I do so envy you, Judy. When you're going somewhere nothing happens to stop you !

JUDY (*sits on* R. *arm of the settee*). My child, I'd give a good deal if something would happen to stop me going where I've got to go to-morrow.

EVE. Your new school ? Who's the Head ?

JUDY. Name of Philpott. Second in command, Miss Mandrill.

EVE. What are they like ?

JUDY. There's a technical term for them, I think. " Horrific." " We dare you to see them both in the same programme ! "

EVE. Any masters ?

JUDY. Mr. Twemlow, mathematics.

EVE. Old, I suppose ?

JUDY. Like the last chapter of Mr. Chips !

EVE. Have you met any of the girls ?

JUDY. No, but the dirt's been dished to me by a girl I know. (*Counting on her fingers.*) Assorted saps ; film fans ; baby vamps ; teachers' pets and common sneaks. All except Hilda Smithson ; she's a pet *and* a sneak.

EVE. Still, she'd be company. What is the food like ?

JUDY. There's a lot of chat about calories and vitamins, but I expect it will all boil down to shepherd's pie and stewed prunes.

EVE. I adore them both ! Do they work you hard ?

JUDY (*slips down into the sofa*). They won't work me hard, but I believe we're all supposed to take the Higher Certificate. But why all this academic curiosity, my child ? It's morbid !

EVE (*rises and crosses* R.). I wish I'd worked hard and taken the Higher Certificate when I was at St. Anselm's. It might have made me feel more like Jack's intellectual equal. Do you understand ?

JUDY. No.

EVE. What games do you play ?

JUDY. You take your choice. Polo—tiddley-winks—all-in wrestling——

EVE. At St. Anselm's I was captain of lacrosse. Do you play lacrosse ?

JUDY. We do. A hellish pastime.

EVE. Have they got a swimming-bath ?

JUDY. We have. Average temperature, zero. (*Rises and crosses* L.) Let's talk about something else, for Gawd's sake.

EVE (*crosses to* JUDY). Judy, one more question. Do they take day girls ?

JUDY. Yes, from ten till four—for those who have homes. For me it's a life sentence.

(EVE *crosses to* C., *thinking*.)

EVE. Judy, I've got a brainwave.

JUDY. Well ?

EVE. I'm afraid to tell you.

JUDY. Don't be so silly.

EVE. You'll laugh.

JUDY. Of course I shall. Come on, tell me.

EVE. It's marvellous—but no, I can't tell you.

JUDY. Oh, come on ; of course you can.

EVE (*to* R. *of the settee*). All right ! I'm going back to school.

JUDY. What ? What are you talking about ?

EVE. I'm going back to school. I'm going to Tadworthy Lodge as a day-girl.

JUDY. Indeed ? Are you bringing your husband with you ?

EVE. Jack will never know. I won't have to start in the morning till he's out, and I'll be home long before he gets in.

JUDY. Great Scott, I believe she means it !

EVE. Of course I mean it.

JUDY ⎫　　　　⎧ You're crazy, raving, crackers and bats——
EVE ⎬ (*together*). ⎨ It'll be heaven—girls and games and
　　⎭　　　　⎩　　gossip !

JUDY. But you're past all that. You're a married woman.

EVE. Am I ?

JUDY. You're a respectable British matron.

EVE. Who's to know ? I wouldn't enter myself as Lady Brent, would I ?

JUDY. What are you going to call yourself ? Shirley Temple ?

EVE. Why not ? Something like that, anyhow. (*She jumps on* R. *of the settee*.) Come on Judy, help me—it'll be heaps and heaps of fun.

JUDY (*suddenly—climbs on* L. *of the settee*). I'm warming up to this, dearie. It'll be a barrel of fun. After all, you can only get spotted and thrown out. It isn't like doing something shady.

EVE. Shady ? It's highly educational !

JUDY. Here ! (*She takes a form from her case*.) Name—age —name of parent or guardian. Guardian—that's the ticket ! You'll be a poor orphan and Jack can be the guardian.

EVE. That's an idea !

JUDY. Fill it up. Here's a fountain-pen ; let it play. (*She puts the document before* EVE *and hands her a fountain-pen*.)

EVE (*laughing*). What can I call myself ? Smith, Jones, Montgomery——?

JUDY. I know. Call yourself—let me see—Ruby Rogers.

Eve. Why ?

Judy. Like dear Ginger, only a different colour. Sign, please.

Eve (*writing*). Ruby Rogers. (*She looks up and laughs.*) I've done it! Oh—the address! I can't give this one.

Judy. Yes, you can. Care of Sir John Brent, Two-fifty Bryanston Square, W.1. You're his ward, my child.

Eve. But—Ruby Rogers ? Suppose somebody writes to her —here ?

Judy. Tell Jack she's a girl friend having certain letters addressed here to be forwarded. Slight affair with boy friend. Jack won't mind. Now your age. Sixteen.

Eve. But I look more than that, don't I ?

Judy. No, you don't.

Eve. Sixteen. (*At foot of the page now.*) Signature of parent or guardian authorizing this application! I can't forge Jack's handwriting.

Judy. I can. Give that to me. (*She takes the form and scribbles on it.*) It's one of the things I do really well. There. (*She hands* Eve *the form.*)

Eve (*going over to the mirror* R.). But, Judy, I'm sure I don't look sixteen any more. Only a few minutes ago Jack told me I was a woman for the first time.

Judy. That was your frock, my dear.

Eve. Was it ? We'll soon see about that! Let me try yours on.

Judy. Oke ! (*Jumping up.*) Come on, off with this non-sense ! (*She unfastens the back of* Eve's *frock.*)

(*They begin to take off their dresses, bending down and pulling them right over their heads.*)

And if they fit you, my lamb, I'm going to *sell* them to you !

(*At that moment* Graves *enters, carrying the butler's tray.*
   Both girls are chattering eagerly, with their heads enveloped in their skirts, and neither sees him.
   Graves *gives a horrified start and exit.*)

CURTAIN.

To face page 37—"Little Ladyship."]

This illustration is inserted to indicate the uniform worn by the girls. The stage setting does not conform with the directions given in the printed edition of the play.

ACT II

SCENE 1

SCENE.—*The scene is a class-room at Tadworthy Lodge. Down R. is a dais with a table and chair on it, facing L. There are eleven school desks. Four in a row, facing the dais, as in the plan. Doors R. and L. Large french window at back. Blackboard on wall above the teacher's table. Maps, etc., on the walls.*

The desks are all occupied, with one exception, by girls in the Tadworthy uniform. These vary in age from fifteen to eighteen, and are of various types. The following are outstanding :

(1) JUDY.
(3) HILDA SMITHSON (*spectacled and industrious*).
(4) CLAIRE WESTBROOK (*blonde and affected*).
(5) OLIVE WAKEFIELD (*dreamy and aloof*).
(6) AMY BATTERSBY (*fat and gluttonous*).
(7) ANN WELLS (*film-fan*).
(8) JANE HARDY (*captain of games*).
(9) JOAN TIMPSON (*a little girl*).

These are seated as numbered in the plan. No. 2 desk is empty.

At present, however, it is impossible to distinguish one girl from another, as all are wearing gas-masks. MISS PHILPOTT, *the headmistress, is calling their names, seated at the table.* MISS MANDRILL, *her assistant, stands beside her, mask in hand. There are three boxes for gas-masks on each desk.*

MISS PHILPOTT. Westbrook ?
WESTBROOK. Here, Miss Philpott.
MISS PHILPOTT. Battersby ?
BATTERSBY. Here, Miss Philpott.
MISS PHILPOTT. Wakefield ?
WAKEFIELD. Here, Miss Philpott.
MISS PHILPOTT. Louder, please, Wakefield. One of the purposes of this drill is to make it possible to identify each pupil by her voice alone.
WAKEFIELD (*loudly*). Here, Miss Philpott.
MISS PHILPOTT. That is better. Smithson ?
SMITHSON (*loudly*). Here, Miss Philpott.

37

Miss Philpott. That is good. I can always rely on you, Smithson.

(Judy *glares resentfully through her mask at* Smithson.)

Wells ?
WELLS. Here, Miss Philpott.
Miss Philpott. Hardy ?
HARDY. Here, Miss Philpott.
Miss Philpott. Rogers ?

(*No reply.*)

Rogers ?
JUDY. Here, Miss Philpott.
Miss Philpott. Promptly, please. Bingley ?
JUDY (*half-taking off her mask for a moment*). Right here, Miss Philpott !
Miss Philpott. Which is Bingley ?

(Judy *rises at No.* 1.)

Avoid self-advertisement, Bingley : I have warned you of that before.
JUDY. Yes, Miss Philpott.
Miss Philpott. You may sit down.

(Judy *sits.*)

Now, all take off your masks.
Miss Mandrill. One—two—three——

(*The girls do so, placing them in the empty boxes in front of them.*)

JUDY (*wiping her face*). They do make you sweat.
Miss Philpott (*overhearing*). What did you say, Bingley ?
JUDY (*rising*). I said these masks make one perspire, Miss Philpott.
Miss Philpott. Gentlemen perspire, horses sweat. Ladies merely glow.

(Judy *sits down.*)

Hardy and Smithson, collect the masks.

(Hardy *and* Smithson *leave their seats to collect the boxes and hand them all to* Miss Mandrill.)

Miss Mandrill has demonstrated to you the correct method of adjusting them. Do you all understand ?
CHORUS. Yes, Miss Philpott.
Miss Philpott. Very well. I trust we shall never have to use them in actual reality, but we must of course comply with the expressed wishes of the authorities.
CHORUS. Yes, Miss Philpott.

Miss Philpott. Remember you will need them in a few weeks' time, on Speech Day.

Judy (*politely*). Will there be as many speeches as all that, Miss Philpott ?

Miss Philpott (*coldly, not quite sure whether this is intended to be rude or not*). The principal speech will be made, and the prizes presented, by Sir Theodore Mellish, Chairman of St. Barnabas' Hospital. Miss Mandrill, will you kindly return these to the matron's store-room ?

Miss Mandrill. Yes, Miss Philpott. (*She crosses to the door* R.)

(Timpson *rises and opens the door for her.   Exit* Miss Mandrill *with masks,* R.)

Miss Philpott. Now you may revert to your regular time-table. What is your subject this hour ?

Smithson (*rises*). Mathematics, Miss Philpott. (*She sits.*)

Miss Philpott. That reminds me. (*She produces a letter.*) Mr. Twemlow has unfortunately been prostrated by phlebitis——

Judy (*to* Wells). By *what* ?

(Wells *scratches herself delicately.*)

Miss Philpott. And is unlikely to be with us until Monday. His place will be taken by Mr. Budge, who has joined our staff for the time being.   Mr. Budge is a recent graduate of Cambridge University, where he distinguished himself in the Mathematical Tripos.   You will find him a stimulating teacher. (*Rising.*) I will bring him to you.

Judy. Yes, Miss Philpott.

(Miss Philpott *steps down from the desk and crosses* R., *glaring at* Judy *as she passes.   The girls all rise, and* Miss Philpott *exits, patting* Smithson *on the back, who obsequiously opens the door for her.   As the door closes there is a general chorus of relaxation. Some begin to chatter, others to eat sweets out of their desks, etc.*)

Kiddy Timpson—sentry !   (R.)

(Timpson *goes to the door and peers through the keyhole* R.   Ann Wells *produces a copy of a film-magazine from her desk and shows it to* Westbrook, *who is standing up tidying herself.*)

Wells (*sitting on the desk*).   Now listen.   " Ronald Colman is five feet eleven inches tall, weighs a hundred and sixty-five pounds, has black hair and brown eyes.   He was born on the ninth of February, eighteen-ninety-one, in Richmond, Surrey, England." And you said he came from Pittsburg !

(Smithson *has resumed her seat and begun to study her repetition book.*)

JUDY (*noticing* SMITHSON, *without waiting for* WELLS *to finish*). No swotting up rep. here. Scug! (*She takes the book and throws it out of the door* L. SMITHSON *indignantly retrieves it.*)
HARDY (*sitting on the second desk*). I say, Judy, where's your friend Rogers to-day?
JUDY (*standing down* L. *by her desk*). You can search me, ducky.
WESTBROOK. Who answered for her, by the way?
JUDY. I cannot think. What do you want her for, Hardy?
HARDY. Cricket next Saturday.
JUDY. She's usually rather busy on Saturday afternoon.
WESTBROOK. She was quite busy last Saturday afternoon!
HARDY. What do you mean?

(WAKEFIELD *is busy reading at her desk, No. 3, and is suddenly spotted by* JUDY. JUDY *crosses to* WAKEFIELD.)

JUDY (*breaking in*). Is it possible that our Wakers is also swotting at her rep.? What is this Trades Union of ours coming to?

(*All eyes turn to* WAKEFIELD.)

WAKEFIELD (*nervously closing her desk*). It isn't rep., Bingley.
WESTBROOK. Then what is it?
WAKEFIELD. Nothing.
WELLS. Give it to her, Wakers.
FRIEDA. What is it?
TIMPSON. I'll bet it's juicy. (*She stands on the desk.*)
HARDY. Let's have a look.
JUDY. Give it to me, Wakefield.
BATTERSBY. Let's hear it!
JUDY (*imitating* MISS PHILPOTT). Give it to me, Wakefield.

(WAKEFIELD *reluctantly gives the book. All gather round.*)

(*Facing the audience.*) Zippy Stories! Tut-tut! (*She opens the book and reads a few lines.*) Really, Wakefield!
CHORUS. Read it, Judy!

(SMITHSON *is the only one who remains seated at her desk.*)

JUDY (*with exaggerated solemnity*). " Her white arms went up around his neck. The radiance of the moon fell full upon his face as he stopped her mouth with his. ' I lurve you, Steve! ' she said."
TIMPSON (*at the door*). Cave!

(*There is a general scuttle for seats.* MISS PHILPOTT *enters* L. *with* MR. BUDGE, *a sturdy and boyish-looking young man, a little at sea in his present surroundings. They cross to the desk* L. MISS PHILPOTT *above and* BUDGE *below.*)

Miss Philpott. Come in, Mr. Budge. This way. You may resume your seats. These are our candidates for the Higher Certificate. You will find that they work best when strictly supervised. I name no names! Smithson,

(Smithson *rises and sits again.*)

the head of the room, will inform you of their present stage of progress. But first there will be repetition—a part of our daily routine—the recital in the present case of a short passage of English poetry, from—— (*She looks at* Smithson.)

Smithson (*rises*). Gray's Elegy, Miss Philpott. (*She sits.*)

Miss Philpott. Gray's Elegy—which your pupils have committed to memory overnight—(*grimly*) I trust! Pray be seated, Mr. Budge.

(*The door opens* R. *and* Eve *appears furtively, in her school dress.*)

Rogers, who gave you permission to leave the room?

Eve. I didn't leave it, Miss Philpott. I've just come.

Miss Philpott. But you answered to your name a moment ago.

Eve. Did I?

Miss Philpott. If you did not, someone else did. Who?

Judy (*rising*). It was me, Miss Philpott.

Miss Philpott (*reprovingly*). It was I!

Judy. Well, I did it too.

(*General laughter.*)

By mistake. I couldn't hear properly through my gas-mask.

Miss Philpott. Frank admission of a fault is all I ever require, as you know. Resume your seat, Bingley.

(Judy *sits again.*)

(*To* Eve.) Come here, Rogers.

(Eve *crosses to the front of the desk.*)

Why do you arrive at this hour, Rogers?

Eve. I was out very late last night with—with my—guardian; and this morning he kept me in bed—told me to stay in bed—till nine.

Miss Philpott. Under Article Seven of our Constitution, unpunctuality is only excused on production of a satisfactory explanation from parent or guardian. A printed form is provided, which must be initialled. Have you brought one?

(Judy *has taken a printed form from her desk and initialled it. She now passes it quietly to* Eve, *who is standing just in front of her.*)

Eve. Yes, Miss Philpott. (*She advances and lays it on* Miss Philpott's *table.*)

MISS PHILPOTT. Thank you. You may sit down.

(EVE *returns to her seat.*)

(*Handing a plan to* BUDGE.) Here is a plan of the desks, Mr. Budge, which will enable you to identify each pupil by name. We will now proceed with repetition. You shall begin, Rogers.
EVE (*rising, alarmed*). Oh! Where, please?
MISS PHILPOTT. From the beginning—a convenient starting-point, as a rule.

(*Titters.*)

Proceed!

(EVE *stands speechless.*)

Have you neglected to learn this passage?
EVE. Oh no. I've just forgotten the first line.
MISS PHILPOTT. Assist Rogers, Smithson. The opening words only.
SMITHSON (*rises*). The curfew tolls—— (*She sits.*)
MISS PHILPOTT. The curfew tolls——
EVE. The curfew tolls—the curf—(*sticking*)—the—curf——
MISS PHILPOTT. You know what a curfew is, I suppose?
EVE. Oh, yes.
MISS PHILPOTT. Well?
EVE. A bird that makes a noise like a bell.
MISS PHILPOTT. Sit down, Rogers.

(EVE *sits. The girls giggle.*)

During the break you will come to my study, and I will endeavour to make clear to you the outstanding points of difference between a curfew and a curlew. And now, Mr. Budge—

(BUDGE *rises.*)

I have another class-room to visit; perhaps you will kindly continue in my place. Pupils are addressed by their surnames, as in boys' schools.

(*The girls rise as she exits down* R. SMITHSON *rushes to the door to open it.*)

(*Patting her on the back as usual.*) Thank you, Smithson.

(*She goes out* R.)

(*As* SMITHSON *returns to her place* JUDY *puts out her foot and trips her up.*)

SMITHSON (*furiously*). Bingley, you did that on purpose!

(*General laughter.*)

JUDY. Of course I did!

HARDY. Serve you right, too, you suck-up!

SMITHSON. I shall tell Miss Philpott!

(*General babble from the girls.*)

BUDGE. Oy! (*Raising his voice.*) Oy! Look here—you can't do that sort of thing here, you know.

JUDY (*rises*). Oh, but this is one of those schools where we do what we like, Mr. Budge.

HARDY (*rising*). The new method.

JUDY. You mustn't inhibit us. It makes us feel all frustrated.

(*More general babble and everyone starts standing in turn.*)

BUDGE. Sit down, you! And you! (*To* TIMPSON.) Sit down, everybody! And keep on sitting down!

(*All sit.*)

WELLS. I suppose you've never taught girls before, Mr. Budge?

BUDGE. No. Only boys, thank you very much.

WESTBROOK (*coyly*). Were they nice boys?

(*General laughter.*)

BUDGE. They were by the time I'd done with them. You seem a pretty tough bunch, if I may say so.

JUDY. All part of the Tadworthy System, Mr. Budge. Free expression of individuality. You'll get used to it.

BUDGE. The first thing you've got to get used to is holding your little tongues. (*Shouting.*) Quiet, everybody!

(*All the girls put their fingers to their lips, shushing each other.*)

That's better!

(*He coughs, and all the girls imitate.*)

Now we must finish up this bilge—poetry. Which of you would like to kick off? (*He consults the plan.*) Everything seems to point to you for the job, Bingley!

JUDY. Couldn't we all write it out instead, Mr. Budge?

HARDY. It would save so much time; and then we could get on to our mathematics.

JUDY. We hear you're a stimulating teacher. Won't you start stimulating us?

CHORUS. Please, Mr. Budge!

BUDGE. All right. Write out the fourth, fifth, and sixth stanzas.

(*The girls are much pleased at the success of this manœuvre. They get out papers and pencils.* BATTERSBY *bangs her desk.*)

And stop that!

(*All girls start banging desks in turn as* BUDGE *tries to stop them. When they stop*—) That's better !

Start from " Where heaves the turf "—Meanwhile I'll go round with this plan and check up on you.

(*He crosses in front of the desk to the fourth row and reads the names :* " Timpson—Hobbs." *The girls begin to write. There is a good deal of whispering and prompting.* JUDY *brings the book out of the desk and, putting it on her knee furtively, copies.* EVE *is nodding rather sleepily ;* JUDY *turns to her.*)

JUDY. Pst !

(EVE *opens her eyes.*)

" Where heaves the turf in many a mouldering heap——"
EVE (*writing*). Sheep ?
JUDY. *Heap,* you mutt !
EVE. Thanks, darling. (*She continues to write. Presently her head sinks on to her arm.*)
JUDY. What's the matter ?
HARDY. She's half asleep.
EVE. I can hardly keep my eyes open.

(*Meanwhile* BUDGE *has arrived at the third row.*)

BUDGE. Westbrook—Wells. (*To* WAKEFIELD, *who shakes her head and points to* WELLS *in front of her.*) Oh—you're Wells ! Then who are you ?
WAKEFIELD. I'm Wakefield, Mr. Budge.
BUDGE. Thanks.

(*He crosses in front to the desk* L. *and as he passes,* JUDY *trips him up.*)

Did you do that on purpose ?
JUDY. Oh, *no,* Mr. Budge ! I thought you did it ! (*She hurriedly puts her book out of sight.*)
BUDGE (*continues checking*). Battersby—Smithson—Hardy—Wells—— (*He gets to* EVE, *who is asleep. He places his hand on her shoulder, and leans over her.*)
EVE (*sleepily*). Don't, darling.

(*The girls laugh.*)

BUDGE. Is anything the matter ?
EVE (*she sits up suddenly*). Oh, I'm so sorry. I must have dropped off.
BUDGE. How much have you written ?

(EVE *shows him her paper.*)

Is that all ?
EVE. I tried so hard to learn it.

BUDGE. I'm sure you did. (*In a low voice.*) " The rude fore-fathers of the hamlet sleep."

EVE. Thank you so much. (*Writing.*) *How* many ?

BUDGE. Four ! (*He pats* EVE *on the shoulder and goes back to his desk.*)

(BUDGE *returns to the desk.*)

JUDY. He's developed a crush on you, my pet ! Instantaneous !

EVE. Shut up !

JUDY (*whispering*). You've got your wedding-ring on !

(EVE *hastily removes her wedding-ring.*)

BUDGE. Right. Show up !

(*All the girls rise and go to his desk with their papers. On their return several of them take their wrong seats.*)

JUDY. Have we acquitted ourselves satisfactorily, Mr. Budge ?

BUDGE (*glancing through the papers*). No, little optimist, you have not. I say, let's call this a wash-out, shall we, and get on to something rather more up my street ? What about a spot of arithmetic ? (*He drops the papers into the waste-paper basket.*) Can you all do proportion ?

CHORUS. What's that, please ?

BUDGE. Oh, comic problems about six men mowing seven fields in three days—and taps filling baths—and what-not. Take this one down, and have a shot.

(*The girls take paper and pencil.*)

Er—if the hot tap of a bath can fill the bath in ten minutes, and the cold tap in five, how long would it take to fill the bath when both taps are turned on ?

JUDY. Is the plug out—or any cad's catch of that kind ?

BUDGE. No. (*To* BATTERSBY, *who has held up her hand.*) Well ?

BATTERSBY (*rising*). We've only got a geyser at our house, Mr. Budge, and it leaks. Does it make any difference ?

BUDGE. No, Timpson, it does not.

TIMPSON (*rising*). I'm Timpson, Mr. Budge.

BUDGE. You were sitting somewhere else a moment ago. (*He consults the plan.*)

TIMPSON. But I'm still Timpson, Mr. Budge.

BUDGE (*rises*). You're in your wrong place in the plan.

TIMPSON. I'm so sorry. I'll change back. (*She does so.*)

WESTBROOK. I'm afraid I'm in my wrong place too ; I didn't know you minded.

(*They all change back to their right places.* JUDY *leans over and talks to* EVE.)

BUDGE (*coming down with his ruler, threatens* JUDY). Sit down, *everybody* ! If you were boys I'd know exactly what to do about this—and I'm not sure I won't do it. And I know where I'll start ! (*To* JUDY, *shouting.*) Sit down, you ! (*He pokes* JUDY *with the ruler.*)

JUDY. Oh, I'm so sorry, Mr. Budge. I do beg your pardon.

(JUDY *sits hastily, and all write industriously for a moment.*)

BUDGE. Has anybody worked out the answer yet ?

(EVE *holds up her hand.*)

Ah—Rogers—good girl !

EVE (*rises*). Please, Mr. Budge, how full is full ?

BUDGE. How what ?

EVE. Full. Has one to fill the bath right up to the brim ?

BUDGE. Always—in arithmetic books !

EVE. Then how does one get into the bath without spilling a lot of it ?

(*All the girls laugh.*)

BUDGE. What are you silly kids laughing at ? It was a most intelligent question.

(JUDY *turns and grins meaningly at* EVE. *A bell rings.*)

What is that bell ?

HARDY (*rises*). Eleven-thirty break, Mr. Budge. Your hour is over.

BUDGE (*to* SMITHSON). Is that right ?

SMITHSON (*rises*). It is quite in order, Mr. Budge.

BUDGE. All right. You can shin out. (*He collects his books.*)

(*The girls rise.* TIMPSON, WELLS, WAKEFIELD, SMITHSON, *go out* R. WESTBROOK *goes out* L. *All talking.*)

(BUDGE *goes towards the door* R. *He passes* EVE, *who is sitting alone at her desk. He smiles at her and goes out* R.)

(HARDY *comes to* EVE, *who is eating sandwiches.*)

HARDY (*sitting on the second desk*). Rogers, I shall want you on Saturday. I'm going to try you against St. Anselm's.

EVE. St. Anselm's ! Oh, I couldn't !

HARDY. But you're good. I saw you bowling at a net yesterday.

EVE. It isn't that. I used to be at St. Anselm's. I can't go back there.

HARDY. Why not ? You weren't sacked, or anything, like Bing ?

EVE. Well—Saturday afternoon is awkward for me, any-how. I—they want me at home. (*She rises.*) Good gracious,

I've just remembered—I've got to see the Philpott about a curlew! I'm so sorry about Saturday, Hardy. (*She goes to the
door* R.)

(WESTBROOK *enters* R. *and meets her in the doorway.*)

WESTBROOK.   Hallo, Rogers.   Were you really out at a party
last night ?   Or just showing off, as usual ?

EVE (*coldly*).   I was out with my guardian.   (*She crosses* R.
and stands in the doorway.)

WESTBROOK.   Where ?

EVE.   Buckingham Palace.

(*All laugh.*)

WESTBROOK.   Was that your guardian you were with at the
Bijou Cinema last Saturday afternoon ?

EVE (*coldly*).   You'd like to know, wouldn't you ?

WESTBROOK.   I'm dying to know.   Whoever he was, you
were well dolled up for him.   Clothes—hair—everything.   Our
little Rogers—all Carole Lombard and Rue de la Paix.   And poor
me in this get-up !   Did you see me, by any chance ?

EVE (*deliberately*).   Yes,—I saw both of you.

(*Exit* EVE R.)

(*The room is now empty except for* WESTBROOK, HARDY *and*
JUDY.)

HARDY.   What was the flap about the Bijou ?

WESTBROOK (*sits at her desk*).   Our little Rogers was there, with
a man.   And were they flying high !

HARDY.   How ?

WESTBROOK.   Holding hands, my dear ; and more than once
she had her head on his shoulder !

JUDY (*sits on top of her desk*).   And whose shoulder was *your*
head on ?

WESTBROOK (*haughtily*).   I happened to be there with my
fiancé.

HARDY.   Your *what* ?

JUDY.   How do you spell it ?

WESTBROOK.   We've had an understanding for some time.

JUDY.   Does your nurse know ?

(WESTBROOK *glares at her.*)

HARDY.   Shut up, Bing !   This is a thrill.   Do your people
know, Westy ?

WESTBROOK.   Know ?   They've forbidden him the house !
We have to meet in mouldy places like cinemas and museums.
There'd be the devil if it was found out.

(JUDY *chokes.*)

HARDY. Do you go about with him in your school kit ? It's frightfully risky.

WESTBROOK. I know ; but I have to. I simply daren't go home to change. I'd never get out again. (*She rises and crosses to the door* R.)

(EVE *re-enters* R.)

Oh—you !

(WESTBROOK *sniffs and goes out* R.)

HARDY. Hallo, Rodge ! What happened ?

EVE (*sits at her desk and eats*). Oh, nothing. But the Philpott is concerned about my general progress. Says I'll never get the Higher Certificate at this rate.

JUDY. Do you want to ?

EVE (*emphatically*). Yes.

HARDY. Wants a Higher Certificate, and sniffs at her cricket colours ! Loopy ! Well, chaps, I'm off for a breather before the Science hour. So long.

(*She comes down* C. *and exits.*)

JUDY (*sits closer*). What's the matter, Goggy ?

EVE. Judy, I'm in a mess. Philpott says I must have some private tuition before the exam comes on. That's going to complicate things.

JUDY. Why ?

EVE. The tutor is to come to our house—every evening at six o'clock. Our house !

JUDY. Just when your dear husband gets home ?

EVE. Yes. What am I going to do about that ? Things are difficult enough already.

JUDY. Is Jack beginning to take notice ?

EVE. Yes, and I know he's getting worried, poor angel. Once or twice he has come home unexpectedly, and I haven't been there. I have Higginson all primed up with an alibi for me, but she's a wretched liar. So am I, for that matter.

JUDY. I'm not bad, but it's never easy. The one advantage of being truthful is that you don't have to remember what you said last time.

EVE. I must get that Higher Certificate.

JUDY. What ever for ?

EVE. I told you once—as a surprise for Jack. At the end of this term I want to go to him and say : " Darling, I know you've been wondering about me lately—just a little bit. I've had a kind of idea that you've even had really dark suspicions once or twice."

JUDY. The Infernal Triangle.

EVE. Yes. " Well," I shall say, " you've been quite gorgeously wrong. Where do you think I've been all this time ? In the place you fished me out of to begin with—school ! Just school ! " Won't it be a divine surprise ?

JUDY. It'll be a divine relief for the poor man, if he's really beginning to smell a rat. But of course it'll mean the end of all this for you. (*She indicates the class-room.*) Are you getting tired of it ?

EVE. Not one bit.

JUDY. I say, you scored off Westy with that crack of yours about Buckingham Palace. Where were you really last night ?

EVE. Buckingham Palace. Presented, on my marriage.

JUDY. Oh, golly ! (*She gives a mock curtsy.*)

(*Enter* MISS PHILPOTT R., *followed by* BUDGE. *Both stop* C. JUDY *and* EVE *both rise.*)

MISS PHILPOTT. Is Rogers here ? Ah—fortunate. Rogers, I have solved our little problem more quickly than I anticipated.

EVE. What problem, Miss Philpott ?

MISS PHILPOTT. Of tuition. Mr. Budge is disengaged in the evenings, and has most kindly undertaken to visit you four times a week, in your own home.

EVE (*faintly*). Oh, thank you, Miss Philpott. Thank you, Mr. Budge.

MISS PHILPOTT. You had better make a personal business arrangement with Mr. Budge, according to our sensible Tadworthy custom.

EVE. But, Miss Philpott. I—I shall have to consult my guardian first.

MISS PHILPOTT. Your guardian will not object to your making the best possible use of your time here.

EVE. No, of course not——

(*Enter* MISS MANDRILL *from* L.)

MISS MANDRILL. Miss Philpott, Mr. Samuel Smithson has called.

MISS PHILPOTT. At this hour of the morning ? (*She crosses to* MISS MANDRILL, L.)

MISS MANDRILL. He says the matter is urgent.

MISS PHILPOTT. Mr. Smithson is a warm friend of the school. If he says a matter is urgent, it is urgent. (*To* MR. BUDGE.) I will leave you together. (*To* MISS MANDRILL.) Is Mr. Smithson in the study ?

MISS MANDRILL. Yes, Miss Philpott.

(MISS PHILPOTT *and* MISS MANDRILL *go out* L.)

JUDY (*crosses* R.). Well, children, I also will leave you together, in accordance with our sensible Tadworthy custom.

(*She coughs loudly and goes out,* R.)

D

EVE (*turning impulsively to* BUDGE). Mr. Budge, I've been thinking. You see, my guardian—he's Sir John Brent, you know, the surgeon—he has patients calling about six ; and well —that means that the consulting-room and the waiting-room and the hall are all crammed with people—and—and——

BUDGE. I suppose Lady Brent requires the drawing-room for herself ?

EVE. Who ? Oh ! Yes—of course ! So you see it would all be rather difficult. I mean, wouldn't it ?

BUDGE. Naturally.

EVE. I could come to you, though.

BUDGE. I'm afraid I only live in two rooms in Belsize Park. That would hardly do, would it ?

EVE. You're not married ?

BUDGE. Gosh, no ! I'm only twenty-three. (*He smiles at* EVE, *obviously wondering how old she is.*) How old are you ?

EVE. About—seventeen. (*She sits on top of the desk.*)

BUDGE (*sits on the bench of the same desk*). I suppose that means that you'll be leaving school soon. (*He sighs.*) And then you'll come out—and be presented at Court—and be what they call a deb, isn't it ?

EVE. Oh, not all at once. There are five stages altogether, you know. For a year you're only a sub-deb ; then you come out, and for a year you're a full deb. The year after that you're an ex-deb—fading away already.

BUDGE. What are you the year after that ?

EVE. A hag. And the year after that you're L O F H.

BUDGE. What is that ?

EVE. Left On Father's Hands !

(*They laugh.*)

BUDGE. I don't think there's much danger of that happening to you.

EVE. It's sweet of you to say so.

BUDGE. But it's true.

EVE (*smiles down at him. They touch hands, shyly. Collecting herself again*). About this tuition. How are we to manage ?

BUDGE. Let me think !

EVE. I've just had another idea. This is a funny school, and we are encouraged to do things in funny ways.

BUDGE. Yes, I've noticed that. Well ?

EVE. Supposing you coach me in funny places ?

BUDGE. How funny ?

EVE. Well, we might go for a stroll on Hampstead Heath, and you could explain Algebra to me, and set me some homework ; and I would do it, and post it to you ; and then we could meet in a tea-shop, perhaps, and you could show me your corrections. Or we might spend a half-holiday up the river, and have a good go at Trigonometry in a backwater somewhere. How does that sound ?

BUDGE. Don't say it again ; I might wake up !

EVE (*rises*). Then you'll do it ? (*Offering her hand.*) **It's a** bargain ?

BUDGE (*holding her hand*). Oh, Miss Rogers !

EVE. You can call me E—Ruby—if you like.

BUDGE. Ruby !

(*The bell rings. Girls are heard returning.*)

I must get out of here ! (*He hurries to the door*, R.)

EVE. We've never settled what you're going to charge. How much ?

(*He has gone. The girls are chattering and resume their seats.*)

JUDY. What do we do at this hour ?

EVE. Electricity and Magnetism.

JUDY. I wish it was Chemistry ; then something might blow up.

TIMPSON (*at the door* R.). Cave. (*She bolts into her seat.*)

MISS MANDRILL *enters from* R., *carrying certain apparatus. She crosses to her desk* L. *The girls have all risen on her entrance. She nods at them and they all sit.*)

MISS MANDRILL. In a few moments we shall adjourn to the Physics Laboratory, where you will perform certain elementary experiments in plotting a magnetic field of force. Last week, you may remember, we discovered that a bar-magnet can attract to itself iron and steel objects—iron filings, for instance. (*She dips a bar-magnet into a heap of iron filings and shows the filings adhering thickly to the magnet.*)

WESTBROOK (*to her neighbour*). Disgusting !

(*Enter* MISS PHILPOTT *from* L. *All the girls rise.*

MISS PHILPOTT (*at the door* L.). Come in, Mr. Smithson.

(MISS PHILPOTT *stands back as* MR. SMITHSON *enters* L. *He is a severe-looking man in horn spectacles.*)

I am sorry to disturb the class a second time this morning, but the sooner we deal with this matter the better. (*She crosses up to the dais.*) You may resume your seats. (*Addressing the girls from behind the table on the dais.*) I regret to say that last Saturday afternoon a girl wearing the Tadworthy uniform was observed behaving in a most unbecoming and unworthy manner in the Bijou Cinematograph Theatre, in Upper Baker Street, W.1. There can have been no mistake, for my informant, Mr. Smithson, is himself the parent of a member of the School, so the uniform is familiar to him. Mr. Smithson tells me that he is not addicted to

this particular form of entertainment, but had merely—er—
dropped in to witness a News Reel—depicting a foundation-stone
laying for which his firm had supplied the mortar. He had
hardly taken his seat when he witnessed a very different scene,
in the auditorium itself! Unfortunately, owing to the subdued
light, he was unable to distinguish the features of the offender—or
rather offenders, for one of them was a man—

(*General sensation.*)

but the Tadworthy uniform was unmistakable. I am here to
discover the culprit. The younger girls, of course, can be ruled
out of the inquiry ; so, as it happens, can the Sixth form, who
were all engaged that afternoon upon a botanizing excursion in
Ken Wood, supervised by the Junior Science Mistress, Miss
Trotter. This narrows our inquiry to yourselves—with one
exception. (*To* HILDA SMITHSON.)

(SMITHSON *rises.*)

Smithson, your father informs me that on Saturday afternoon
you took a brisk walk across Clapham Common with your mother.
You may withdraw.

SMITHSON. Thank you, Miss Philpott.

(*She goes out in front of the desk, passing* JUDY *carefully. The girls
all glare at her.*)

MISS PHILPOTT. Now ! (*She looks round the room expectantly.*)

(*The girls glance at one another covertly.* WESTBROOK *is obviously
ill at ease.*)

As you know, it is my practice to deal as leniently as possible
with a voluntary admission of guilt. Of course, I cannot make
any promises on this occasion. Has anyone anything to say
to me ?

(*There is silence.*)

I am disappointed. (*She looks round again.*) Very well, I must
question you individually. Bingley, where were you on Saturday
afternoon last, between the hours of three and five ?

JUDY (*rising*). At Lord's, Miss Philpott—with my old—my
father.

MISS PHILPOTT. You were witnessing a game of cricket ?

JUDY. I was. My father was asleep.

MISS PHILPOTT. Avoid irrelevant detail at all times, Bingley

JUDY. Yes, Miss Philpott. (*She sits down.*)

MISS PHILPOTT. Hardy !

HARDY (*rising*). Yes, Miss Philpott ?

MISS PHILPOTT. Where were you ?

HARDY. Playing cricket.

MISS PHILPOTT (*with grim humour*). Not upon Lord's Cricket-ground, I presume.

HARDY. No, Miss Philpott.

(*The girls laugh. MISS PHILPOTT motions to them to stop.*)

Against St. Hilda's, at Wimbledon.

MISS PHILPOTT. Quite in order. How many of you were similarly engaged ?

(*Two hands go up.*)

Wakefield—Hobbs—thank you. Battersby, where were you ?

BATTERSBY (*a fat girl*). I went to the confectionery exhibition at Olympia, Miss Philpott.

MISS PHILPOTT. Wells ?

(HARDY *sits.*)

WELLS (*rising*). I went to see Anna Neagle open a fancy fair at Cricklewood, Miss Philpott—in person !

MISS PHILPOTT. Who is the lady in question ?

ALL. A film star, Miss Philpott.

MISS PHILPOTT (*ironically*). I am always happy to have my astronomical horizon enlarged. Westbrook ?

(WELLS *sits.*)

WESTBROOK (*rising nervously*). I went for a walk, Miss Philpott.

MISS PHILPOTT. Unaccompanied ?

WESTBROOK. Yes—quite.

MISS PHILPOTT. Was that not a little unsociable of you ? You have brothers and sisters.

WESTBROOK. I like to be alone.

MISS PHILPOTT. Where did you walk ?

WESTBROOK. In Kensington Gardens.

MISS PHILPOTT. Very healthy and invigorating. About what time ?

WESTBROOK. From about three till fire.

MISS PHILPOTT (*rises*). Indeed ! Then how is it that shortly after three o'clock you were observed by Miss Mandrill walking —almost loitering—along Oxford Street ?

WESTBROOK. I wasn't loitering, Miss Philpott. I was doing some shopping—for my mother.

MISS PHILPOTT. On a Saturday afternoon, in Oxford Street ? Have you ever heard of the Shop Hours Act, Westbrook ?

WESTBROOK. I'd forgotten about it being early-closing day.

MISS PHILPOTT. And your mother had been guilty of the same oversight ? Very strange. I suppose your mother can corroborate your statement ?

(WESTBROOK *looks terrified.* EVE *turns and looks at her.*)

You appear to be uncertain on the point.   Miss Mandrill, would
you be so kind as to telephone—to Mrs. ——
WESTBROOK (*frantically*).   Please——

(MISS PHILPOTT *signals to* WESTBROOK *to sit down.* WESTBROOK
sinks into her seat.)

MISS PHILPOTT.   Well, Rogers ?
EVE (*rising*).   It's all right, Miss Philpott.   I was the one.
MISS PHILPOTT.   The one what, Rogers ?
EVE.   I was the girl in the Bijou Cinema.   I've been trying
to own up for the last five minutes, I'm terribly sorry.

(*There is an astonished silence.   Then—*)

MISS PHILPOTT.   You mean what you say ?
EVE.   Yes.
MISS PHILPOTT.   You are speaking the absolute truth ?
EVE.   Absolutely.
MISS PHILPOTT.   The inquiry need go no further, so far as the
rest of you are concerned.   Please accept my regrets that you
should have been subjected to suspicion in the first place.   You
will all withdraw to the outer hall for a few moments, except
Rogers.

(*The girls go out, obviously disappointed at missing the final scene.*
WESTBROOK *goes last, looking at* EVE.   *The door closes.*   MISS
PHILPOTT, *coming down from the dais, stands in front of* EVE.
SMITHSON *looks over her shoulder.*)

Let us be *quite* clear about this.   You deliberately confess to
having attended a public entertainment in the Tadworthy
uniform, and to having there behaved in an unseemly manner
with a young man !
EVE.   There wasn't anything very unseemly about it, Miss
Philpott—and he wasn't a young man at all.   He was my—
guardian.
MISS PHILPOTT.   Sir John Brent ?
EVE.   Yes.
MR. SMITHSON (*speaking for the first time*).   You kissed him !
EVE.   Nonsense !
MR. SMITHSON.   But I saw you !
EVE (*to* MISS PHILPOTT).   I don't care what Mr. Smithson
thinks he saw.   I rather think he's one of those people who
always see what they're looking for, whether it's there or not.
All I did was to hold my guardian's hand ; and once or twice,
during the sentimental bits, (*smiles*) I think I put my head on his
shoulder !

Miss Philpott. You must be very devoted to your guardian.

Eve. I am : he's an angel. He takes me about with him quite a lot.

Miss Philpott. Where is Lady Brent upon these occasions ?

Eve. Lady Brent ? Oh, she comes too.

Miss Philpott. But she was not present upon this occasion ?

Eve. Oh yes, she was.

Miss Philpott (to Smithson). Did you see Lady Brent, Mr. Smithson ?

Mr. Smithson. I haven't the honour of knowing her ladyship by sight.

Eve. Would you care to ring her up and ask her, Miss Philpott ? She'll be at home about six, I know.

Miss Philpott. It will not be necessary. I accept your word, and I am willing to believe, that in the obscurity of the auditorium, Mr. Smithson's eyesight was—shall we say ?—a little more than equal to the occasion. Miss Mandrill, will you be so kind as to see Mr. Smithson out ? (She shakes hands with Mr. Smithson coldly.) Thank you for your more than zealous interest in the moral welfare of my pupils. Good morning.

(Mr. Smithson looks as if he would like to protest ; then thinks better of it and follows Miss Mandrill out L.)

Nevertheless, Rogers, I must take formal notice of your indiscretion. You will write out, in copperplate, twenty-five times : (Eve takes paper and writes) " Public demonstrations of affection, however legitimate, by a wearer of the Tadworthy uniform, are at variance with the Tadworthy Tradition." Have you got that ?

Eve. Yes, Miss Philpott.

Miss Philpott. Correctly ?

(Eve has been scribbling down the words at her desk.)

Eve (rises). Yes, Miss Philpott.

Miss Philpott. You will hand it to Miss Mandrill before first school to-morrow.

(She goes out L.)

(Westbrook appears R. and throws herself on Eve's neck.)

Westbrook. Darling—angel—bless you ! You don't know what you've got me out of ! (She kisses her frantically.) It was grand of you to do it—divine—after I'd been so foul to you !

Eve. All right, all right ! (She crosses to the door R.)

Westbrook. Why did you do it ?

Eve. I don't know.

WESTBROOK. I do. You're in love with some one yourself!
You must be, to behave like that. Are you?

(EVE *nods gravely.*)

But—*not* with your guardian?
EVE. No, dear, not with my guardian!

CURTAIN.

(*Quick change to Scene* 2.)

SCENE 2

SCENE.—*The hall of the house in Bryanston Square again. One
evening, a few weeks later.*

As the CURTAIN *rises* GRAVES *enters* C. *from* R. *and crosses to the
front door* L. *and exit.*
As GRAVES *exits,* HIGGINSON *appears* C. *from* R., *looks round
cautiously and speaks off to* EVE.

HIGGINSON. All right, you can come in.

(EVE *appears from* R. *in school dress, carrying a despatch-case.*)

EVE. What should we do without our side door? (*She goes
to the consulting-room door* R. *and listens.*)
HIGGINSON. I'll go upstairs first. That nosey new house-
maid's there. (*She goes off up* L.)

(GRAVES' *voice is heard off* L. *talking to* MRS. BINGLEY. EVE
bolts after HIGGINSON.)

GRAVES (*off stage*). Good afternoon, madam.

(*Enter* MRS. BINGLEY, *shown in by* GRAVES.)

MRS. BINGLEY. Good afternoon, Graves. How have you
been keeping? And Mrs. Graves?
GRAVES. Very well, thank you, madam. (*He shuts the down-
stage door* L.)

(*He exits up* R.)

(SIR JOHN *enters from the consulting-room* R., *crosses to* C. *and
shakes hands with* MRS. BINGLEY.)

MRS. BINGLEY. Hallo, John!
SIR JOHN. Good afternoon, Cynthia. Back from Aix! I
hope Kenneth's health has profited.
MRS. BINGLEY. If it has, he's keeping it a secret. How are
you?
SIR JOHN. Overworked, but no complaints.

MRS. BINGLEY (*crosses to the front of the settee*). And her little Ladyship ? Where is she ?

SIR JOHN. Her maid informed me when I came in half an hour ago that she was having a nap.

MRS. BINGLEY. At her age ? (*She sits* L. *end of the settee.*)

SIR JOHN. She's had a long day. Do you know, I rang her up from the hospital at half-past nine this morning and she was out already ? There's energy for you !

MRS. BINGLEY. My good man, come to the point. How have things been going since I saw you a month ago ? That party. Did you get tight, as I told you ?

SIR JOHN. That particular party had to be postponed.

MRS. BINGLEY. How dared you ?

SIR JOHN. Unavoidable. A very urgent telephone call at the eleventh hour—critical operation, and so on. But the party came off all right—quite successfully, three days later. Thank you, Cynthia.

MRS. BINGLEY. What for ?

SIR JOHN. For gingering me up. I *was* neglecting her, you know—taking her a little too much for granted. Will you have some tea ? (*He rises.*)

MRS. BINGLEY. I had it an hour ago. Tell me more.

SIR JOHN. Well. (R. *of the settee*). We go out together quite a lot now. We dance—think of that ! Me ! I know what swing is (*swings his leg and finds it stiff*)—at least, I think so !

MRS. BINGLEY. Has she discovered what married women do in the daytime ? Last time I saw her she didn't know.

SIR JOHN. Oh, she's quite busy nowadays. So busy that she's often quite glad of a quiet evening at home.

MRS. BINGLEY. What keeps her busy ?

SIR JOHN. A lot of silly things, she says.

MRS. BINGLEY. What sort of silly things ?

(*The telephone rings.*)

SIR JOHN. Excuse me. (*He goes to the telephone* R. *and answers.*) Who ? Julie, Dover Street ? (*He looks puzzled.*)

MRS. BINGLEY. Hairdresser.

SIR JOHN. Thank you. Yes ? (*He listens.*) You are sorry to have had to disappoint her Ladyship this morning, but Miss Melanie will keep free and attend to her specially at six this evening. Thank you ; I will tell her. We must wake her up presently. (*He crosses to the table behind the settee and scribbles the message on a pad.*)

MRS. BINGLEY (*steadily*). What sort of silly things ?

SIR JOHN. That she never seems to be able quite to explain. She's a vague young woman.

MRS. BINGLEY. She used not to be.

SIR JOHN. Anyhow, she has learned to occupy herself in one

direction. She has taken to writing—in a rather clandestine way. At first I thought it must be poetry.

MRS. BINGLEY. Much more likely an illicit correspondence, my dear.

SIR JOHN. Are you suggesting——? (*He crosses to* R. *of the settee.*)

MRS. BINGLEY. She must have taken my advice, and picked up a young man somewhere.

SIR JOHN. Your advice ?

MRS. BINGLEY. Yes ; I wrote from Aix, and suggested it. Nothing serious, of course : I stressed that. Something just sufficient to pass the time, and keep you guessing.

(SIR JOHN *produces a paper from his pocket.*)

What's that ?

SIR JOHN. I picked it up off the floor, quite casually, one evening last week. (*He hands the paper to* MRS. BINGLEY.) It doesn't sound particularly ardent.

MRS. BINGLEY (*reading*). " Public demonstrations of affection, however legitimate, by a wearer of the Tadworthy uniform, are at variance with the Tadworthy tradition. Public demonstrations——" It starts all over again, then stops suddenly.

SIR JOHN. Why ? What is the Tadworthy uniform, do you suppose ?

MRS. BINGLEY. Tadworthy Lodge is the name of the school to which I send my criminal child, Judy. Don't you remember I read you some extracts from the constitution only a few weeks ago ?

SIR JOHN. Oh, yes, I remember now.

MRS. BINGLEY. This is probably Judy's—though why she should indulge in public demonstrations of affection for anybody at all beats me. She dropped this some time when she was visiting Eve, that's all. (*She places the paper on the table behind.*)

SIR JOHN. But she's always writing nowadays, on foolscap and in note-books ! She hustles them out of sight when I come into the room. I'm going to tackle her on the subject to-night.

MRS. BINGLEY. You'll get no change out of her, my dear.

SIR JOHN. What'll you bet ?

MRS. BINGLEY. Sixpence.

SIR JOHN. Taken.

(*The telephone rings.*)

MRS. BINGLEY. See who that is. It may be the boy friend himself !

SIR JOHN (*crossing to the telephone* R.). Hallo ! Yes. (*To* MRS. BINGLEY.) This is for me !

MRS. BINGLEY. Professional ?

SIR JOHN. Highly. I'll have to take this call in the other room. (*Through the telephone.*) Hold on !

MRS. BINGLEY. I'm scramming, anyhow. I have to collect Ken from a Turkish bath. I'll look in for a moment later, and see Eve. By the way, it's Speech Day at Tadworthy to-morrow. My warrior husband is helping Sir Theo Mellish to inspect the School Gas Corps. Why not come along and have a good laugh ?

SIR JOHN. I'll ask Eve.

MRS. BINGLEY. Right. I'll let myself out. (*She crosses to the door* L.) You'll lose your bet.

(*She exits* L.)

(SIR JOHN *picks up the paper from the table behind the settee, crosses to the consulting-room and exits.*)

(EVE *appears* C., *followed by* HIGGINSON. EVE *crosses to the table* L.C. *and lights a cigarette. She has changed her school clothes for something more suitable.*)

EVE. Higgie, I suppose you don't know anything about quadratic equations ?

HIGGINSON (*crosses to* R. *of the table*). No, nor want to. They don't sound respectable to me.

EVE. They come in Algebra. They're disgustingly difficult. There are two to-day that simply won't come out, and I have to meet my tutor at six. (*She crosses to the settee and sits* L. *end.*)

HIGGINSON. That Fudge ?

EVE. Budge.

HIGGINSON. Where are you going to meet him this time ?

EVE. We've found a new place—a great improvement. One simply can't do Algebra at the Corner House.

HIGGINSON. Where's this one ?

EVE. The tea-room at the Bijou Cinema. It's handy for here, and nearly empty at six.

HIGGINSON. Sir John rang you up from the hospital this morning.

EVE. Oh !

HIGGINSON. Three times in twenty minutes. A nice lot of lies I had to think of.

EVE. Never mind, Higgie darling ; you're improving every day. (*She sits on the settee and starts up again.*) Heavens, I'd forgotten ! My lines ! I wrote out twenty-five lines on Tuesday evening, and I lost them by Wednesday morning. Have you found them ?

HIGGINSON. No !

EVE. Perhaps Graves——?

HIGGINSON. He hasn't said anything to me.

(EVE *crosses to the desk up* C. *and takes out a paper and pen. She sits at the chair above the table.*)

EVE. Isn't that awful ! It means I'll have to start all over again. (*She starts writing and quotes.*) " Public demonstrations of affection, however legitimate——"

HIGGINSON. Nothing's legitimate in this house.

(*Exit* HIGGINSON *by the door up* R.)

EVE (*continues*). "—by a wearer of the Tadworthy uniform," etcetera.

(*Enter* SIR JOHN R. *He crosses to the telephone and puts the receiver back.*)

(EVE *slides the paper off the table, and as* SIR JOHN *turns his back she quickly jumps up and, hiding the paper behind the cushion on the settee, she crosses to meet* SIR JOHN C.)

Hullo, angel—I thought you were with a patient ! Good morning ! (*She kisses him.*)—and good afternoon ! (*She kisses him again.*)

SIR JOHN. And good evening !

EVE. I hear you rang me up this morning. I'm so sorry I was out. I was at the hairdresser's. Was it something important ? A surprise ? A treat ?

SIR JOHN. Well, that's for you to say. I've been offered two stalls to-night for the Russian Ballet.

EVE. I should adore it. (*She crosses to the table, speaking slowly.*) But I may not be back in time.

SIR JOHN. You're not going out now ?

EVE (*puts out her cigarette*). In a few minutes—the dressmaker.

SIR JOHN. Why can't the dress be sent here ?

EVE (*sits* R. *of the settee*). It's the final fitting, darling. I must go there. And I'm a bit tired to-night, anyhow. Can't we stay at home and have a nice, cosy evening together ?

SIR JOHN. I'm always ready to meet you half-way there.

EVE. I know. It's sweet of you.

SIR JOHN (*crosses to behind the table and lights a cigarette*). Cynthia was here a moment ago. She asked me if we'd like to go to Speech Day at Judy's school to-morrow.

(EVE *is startled.*)

Sir Theodore Mellish is inspecting the Gas Corps, and Kenneth will be standing by his side.

EVE. Oh ! that would be no fun for you, darling.

SIR JOHN. Perhaps not. School-girls in gas-masks—what a world !

EVE. Miss Philpott is very keen on A.R.P.

SIR JOHN (*crosses to* L. *of the settee*). Who is Miss Philpott ?

EVE. It's the name of the Headmistress. Judy told me. Once a week they put on gas-masks, and carry each other about on stretchers.

SIR JOHN. I should like to see Judy in a gas-mask—permanently, if possible. (*He sits next to* EVE.) Eve, let's go.

EVE. Oh no, my lamb, I couldn't.

SIR JOHN. Why not ?

EVE (*hesitating*). It won't interest *us*, will it ?

SIR JOHN. Nonsense ! It'll be fun. Come on !

EVE. No, no, please ! I couldn't. I am doing something else, anyhow. Yes, I thought so. (*She looks at his wrist-watch.*) I must fly. My appointment's at six. (*She rises and runs up the stairs.*)

SIR JOHN. Talking of appointments—I'd forgotten something. (*He picks up the pad from the table.*) Here's a telephone message for you from—— (*Suddenly.*) Wait a minute. This is rather odd.

EVE. What's the matter, dear ?

SIR JOHN. Didn't you say you were at the hairdresser's this morning ?

EVE. Yes, of course. Yes. I had a permanent wave. (*Nervously.*) What is it ?

SIR JOHN (*rises and crosses to the foot of the stairs. Reading from the pad*). Julie says she's sorry she had to disappoint you this morning, but somebody called Miss Melanie will keep herself free and attend to you especially at six this evening. (*He looks hard at* EVE.)

EVE (*crosses to above the table* L.C. *Hurriedly*). It must be a mistake of the girl who works the telephone and makes the dates. You see, at first Julie said they couldn't take me, but in the end they did. I expect they forgot to tell the telephone girl, and—well—she arranged this second appointment for me, not knowing. That's all. (*Putting the pad on the table, she smiles up at him. She is not quite sure of the success of her story.*)

SIR JOHN (*down* C., *calmly*). I should keep that second appointment if I were you.

EVE. What do you mean ?

SIR JOHN. You need it. (*He crosses to* EVE.) Eve dear, I am only a humble male, but I do know a permanent wave when I see one. That mop of yours—look at it ! (*He takes her by the shoulders and pushes her gently in front of a mirror on the wall* R.) That was never attended to this morning. If it was, I should sack Miss Melanie. (L. *of* EVE.) Eve, own up ! Where were you this morning ?

EVE (*crosses below* SIR JOHN *to* R. *of the table* C.). What makes you think I was anywhere ?

SIR JOHN (C.). I rang you up three times this morning. The first time you were still in bed. I gave you ten minutes and rang again. You were said to be in your bath. I gave you another ten minutes and rang again. You were out. And Higginson did nothing but stutter every time she heard my voice.

EVE (*stuttering*). But—but—but——

SIR JOHN. You're doing it now !

EVE (*to* SIR JOHN). But—but why shouldn't I go out ? What's the matter with you ?

SIR JOHN. I'll tell you. I'm rapidly becoming a bigamist. I seem to gave acquired two wives of late. One is beautiful and tender and adorable ; the other is a little furtive creature who's always hiding papers and scurrying out of one door as I come in by another. Eve, what's the mystery ?

EVE (*turns up stage*). Darling, there's no mystery at all—really.

SIR JOHN (*catches hold of her arm and turns her round*). What were you writing when I came in ?

EVE. Nothing that would interest you.

SIR JOHN (*puts her on the table*). Eve, you're lying !

EVE. Well, don't look so grim about it. I'm always telling lies, especially to people I love. The more I love a person, the bigger the lie. I think it's called a complex, or something.

SIR JOHN. Is it ?

EVE. Yes. But now I'm going to tell you the truth. I was not at the hairdresser's this morning : I was at the dressmaker's.

SIR JOHN. Janet Joy, Berkeley Street ?

EVE. That's right. How clever of you to remember !

SIR JOHN. Most husbands have good reason to remember names like that. But why must you visit the good lady twice in the same day ?

EVE. The frock wasn't quite right this morning. This is a final fitting. That's all.

SIR JOHN (*stepping back*). But why all the mystery ? Why in heaven's name didn't you say so ?

EVE. Because I wanted the frock to be a surprise to you, darling. It's a dream. You like me to look nice and alluring, don't you ?

SIR JOHN. Heaven forgive me for a wicked old man, I do !

EVE (*kisses him*). Promise you'll trust me in future ?

SIR JOHN. Certainly, if you'll trust me.

EVE. But I always trust you. (*She runs up* R.)

SIR JOHN (*steps to the end of the table and turns up stage*). Very well then, Eve, tell me what you were writing on that paper.

EVE. Oh, are we back there again ? (*She comes back and sits on the* R. *arm of the settee. Playing for time.*) Very well, then, you guess, and I'll tell you if you're right. Come on—ask me questions. You won't guess the real answer.

SIR JOHN (*to* R.C.). Won't I ? Is it poetry ?

EVE. No.

SIR JOHN. Prose ?

EVE. I shan't tell you.

Sir John (*he crosses below* Eve *and kneels on the settee* L. *of her*). It's prose. A novel ? A play ? An essay ?

(Eve *shakes her head.*)

A letter to somebody ?

Eve. It's not a letter, but you're a little warmer.

Sir John. Then it was for somebody. Man or woman ?

Eve. I shan't tell you that !

Sir John. Well, what is it about ?

Eve. It's about—er—twenty-five lines.

Sir John. Eve, stop playing the fool !

Eve. It is about twenty-five lines. Why should I write more —when Philpott . . .

Sir John. When—what ?

Eve. When I've said all I have to say. Would you ?

Sir John. Yes—No—— (*He rises and pulls* Eve *up*.) Eve —for the last time—will you come down to earth and tell me what you were writing ?

Eve. For the last time—No ! (*Throwing his arm off.*)

Sir John. Yes !

Eve. No !

(*Enter* Graves *from the pantry up* R.)

Sir John. Is that a patient, Graves ?

Graves. It's the patients' bell, Sir John.

(Eve *takes the opportunity to escape and exits up* R.)

Sir John (*runs and calls after her*). Eve, I'll be waiting for you when you come down. I'll get that answer out of you before you leave this house.

(Graves *opens the doors down* R. *for* Sir John, *who goes into the consulting-room.* Graves *crosses to the door* L. Eve *appears again with hat, gloves, and handbag.*)

Eve. As soon as you've shown that patient in, Graves, I want you. (*She is about to exit when she remembers the paper under the cushion, which she takes with her, off* R., *towards the pantry.*)

(Graves *opens the front door.* Colonel Bingley *appears* R., *followed by* Mrs. Bingley, *who crosses to above the table* L.C.)

Colonel (*to* C. *below the settee*). Hallo, hallo, where's everybody ?

(Sir John *emerges from the consulting-room.* Graves *goes* R. *into the pantry.*)

Sir John (*to* C.). Oh, Kenneth, it's you !

Mrs. Bingley. Yes, here we are again !

Sir John. I hear you've been having a Turkish bath.

COLONEL. Yes, and I rather think that damned masseur has displaced one of my spinal vertebrae. (COLONEL BINGLEY *exits down* R. *and groans.*)

MRS. BINGLEY. Where's Eve ?

SIR JOHN. Getting ready to go out.

(SIR JOHN *is about to follow* COLONEL BINGLEY *when* HIGGINSON *passes the opening* C., *carrying a large dressmaker's package.*)

What's that, Higginson ?

HIGGINSON. For her Ladyship, Sir John.

MRS. BINGLEY (*crosses to* HIGGINSON). Has she been buying a new frock ? Let me see.

(*She takes the package.* HIGGINSON *looks very guilty.*)

Janet Joy ! How grand !

SIR JOHN (*crosses to* MRS. BINGLEY). Janet Joy ? (*He takes the package and examines it thoughtfully.*) All right, Higginson, give it to her Ladyship.

(HIGGINSON *exits with the package.*)

MRS. BINGLEY. What's the matter ?

SIR JOHN (*pacing up and down*). She's supposed to have a appointment with Janet Joy for six—final fitting or something ! And the dress is here ! (*He is very suspicious.*)

COLONEL (*pokes his head through the door* R.). I say, how much do you want me to take off ?

SIR JOHN. Go on till I tell you to stop !

(*The telephone bell rings.* SIR JOHN *goes and takes off the receiver.*)

Hallo ? Two-fifty, Bryanston Square. (*Impatiently.*) Who are you ? Who ? Spell it. B—U—D— Oh, Budge ? Yes. Mathematical master where ? Tadworthy Lodge. Yes—well ? Miss who ? Podgers ? Oh, Rogers ? Yes ? Miss Ruby Rogers ? I say, what number do you want ? Yes, that's right. Wait a minute ; is she one of the maids here ? She's what ? Whose ward ? (*A slight pause.*) And you're waiting for her at the Bijou Cinema. Hold on, Mr. Budge. I'll give her your message. (*He calls.*) Eve !

(*No answer. He raises his voice.*)

Eve ! (*He turns and calls off* R.) Graves !

(GRAVES *enters* R.)

Graves, do you know where her Ladyship is ?

GRAVES. Her Ladyship has gone out, Sir John.

SIR JOHN (*looking at the front door*). Gone out ?

GRAVES (*very dignified*). Her Ladyship left by the backyard sir. She asked me to give her a leg-up over the wall.

SIR JOHN. Any explanation ?

GRAVES. Her Ladyship offered no explanation.

SIR JOHN. Very well, Graves.

(GRAVES *exits*.)

(*He crosses to the telephone*.) Don't worry, Mr. Budge, she's on her way to meet you now. (*He bangs down the receiver and crosses to* MRS. BINGLEY C.)

MRS. BINGLEY. You've lost your bet.

SIR JOHN. I have, yes. And you're going to see me at the Tadworthy Speech Day, after all.

MRS. BINGLEY. And who are *you* going to make a speech to ?

SIR JOHN (*taking out a cigarette-case*). A young gentleman by the name of *Budge*. (*Taking out a cigarette, he snaps the case closed*.)

CURTAIN.

E

ACT III

SCENE.—*The class-room again on the afternoon of Speech Day. The french windows at the back are opened on to the garden. There is a striped awning over the window outside, denoting festivities of some kind. Distant music. Desks have been cleared away, and the room is decorated with flags, etc. A table is set up* R., *with teetotal refreshments. There are some chairs set about.* MISS PHILPOTT'S *desk is in its usual place, with a vase of flowers on it.* EVE *is discovered hiding under the desk.* JUDY, *in her uniform, appears at the window from* R. *and sidles in furtively. She goes to the table* R. *where teetotal drinks and a plate of sponge-finger biscuits are laid out. She gives a sigh of satisfaction, and after looking off through a door* R., *takes up a glass of Kia Ora and a biscuit and begins to eat.*

EVE (*startled*). Judy!

JUDY (*turning with her hand on her heart*). Oh! I thought you were the Mandrill! But why the Whipsnade act?

EVE. I'm hiding.

JUDY. Who from? (*She crosses to* EVE, *who crawls out to meet her. They kneel on the floor together.*)

EVE. Jack. Jack's here—here! Didn't you see him sitting on the platform, with Uncle Ken and Cynthia?

JUDY (*crosses up to the table* R.). To be quite frank, darling, I gave the speeches a miss. Have some Kia Ora. It's for the platform party, really. (*Bringing down two glasses and a plate of sponge-finger biscuits.*)

EVE. I don't *think* he saw me.

JUDY (*kneels in front of the desk*). Well, he will if you stay here. The entire bunch will be along any minute now.

EVE (*suddenly*). Great heavens! (*She puts down the glass.*)

JUDY. Now what?

EVE. Will Samuel Smithson be with them?

JUDY. Smithson? Is that old purity hound on the premises again? (*She sits on the rug in front of the desk.*)

EVE. Yes; he was sitting in the front row, with his foul daughter.

JUDY. But he's got nothing on you, ducky. Didn't you spike his guns a few weeks ago, over that cinema business?

EVE. Yes; but that was a few weeks ago. I'm thinking of what happened yesterday evening.

66

JUDY. What did happen yesterday evening ? Spill it !

EVE. Smithson paid another visit to the cinema—and he found me there, in the tea-room.

JUDY. With what member of the opposite sex ?

EVE. Budge.

JUDY. I see. A little private tuition was in progress ?

EVE. He was kissing me.

JUDY. Where ?

EVE. On the back of the neck, while I was writing. He'd never done it before.

JUDY. Well, he seems to have picked a good moment for it. What did Smithson say ?

EVE. He asked Budge what he was doing.

JUDY. And Budge said he was sounding you for bronchitis ? But did Smithson recognize you—that's the important point ?

EVE. Only my face. He couldn't remember my name. But he knew Budge, and said he was coming here this afternoon to expose his conduct.

JUDY. Budge should worry ! He's leaving here, anyhow. Got a job somewhere in Suffolk ; he told me.

EVE. Yes, but supposing Smithson asks the Philpott to line us up for an identity parade ?

JUDY. Well, you can only get sacked ; and you can't stay here for ever. You said so yourself.

EVE. But—Jack ! He's been getting terribly suspicious lately. Only last night he started cross-examining me. And if he hears Smithson's story, he might divorce me, or something !

JUDY (rises—takes EVE's glass). Don't get in such a flap ! Nothing is going to happen to you. All you have to do is to keep out of sight for the rest of the afternoon.

EVE. Where ?

JUDY (puts the glasses back on the table behind the settee). Go and sit in the potting-shed or somewhere. And if you have to come out into the open, put your gas-mask on ! (Indicating the gas-mask.) Hallo !

(Someone who has been standing outside the window R. suddenly runs across from R. to L. and disappears. It is HILDA SMITHSON.)

Who was that ? . . . The Smithson girl ! She heard all we said. She'll spill the beans to her old man. We must stop her !

EVE. How ?

JUDY. Death, if necessary !

EVE. Good.

JUDY. Come on !

EVE. But I may run into Jack.

JUDY. No you won't. I'll round him up, and keep him and the family in play. You go and bury the body yourself ; then hide, until people go home.

E*

EVE. Right.

(JUDY *goes up to the window* C. *and looks off, sees her father approaching and signals to* EVE *to go. Exit* EVE *by the window* L.C.)

(*Enter* COLONEL *and* MRS. BINGLEY *from the windows* R.C.)

MRS. BINGLEY. There you are, Judy. Heaven help all platform parties. (*She drops down* R. *and sits in a chair* R.) Thank God for a seat with a cushion on it !

COLONEL (*going up to back where the drinks are on the table*). Thank God for a goblet of moisture ! What are these, Judy ?

JUDY (L. *of the table*). Lemonade, Orangeade, Kia Ora.

COLONEL. *What ?*

JUDY. Kia Ora, Orangeade, Lemonade. (*Picking up a bottle.*) Passion fruit juice !

COLONEL (*moving down* R.). This is the end ! Cynthia, I'm going home.

(JUDY *crosses* L. *and sprawls ungracefully in the chair* R. *of the desk, putting one leg over the arm.*)

MRS. BINGLEY. You must say good-bye to Miss Philpott first. Give me a drink. (*She motions to* JUDY *who promptly swings her other leg over as well.*)

COLONEL. Where is Miss Philpott ? (*Behind the table pouring a drink for* MRS. BINGLEY.)

MRS. BINGLEY. Putting Sir Theodore into his car. Poor old man, he was very tired.

COLONEL. Not half so tired as his audience. All that stuff about schooldays being the happiest time of one's life. Silly old liar ! And what did he mean by telling all those girls that the girl is Mother to the woman ? Doesn't he know that the woman is mother to the girl ? Silly old fool ! (*He presses the soda syphon.*)

(*Enter* MISS PHILPOTT *and* MISS MANDRILL *from* L.C. *They wear gowns, hoods, and mortar-boards.* MISS MANDRILL *stays* L. *of the windows.* JUDY *rises quickly.*)

MISS PHILPOTT (C.). Ah, Colonel, I'm glad to see you have not spared the refreshments. (*She sees* JUDY.) Mrs. Bingley, I'm afraid you cannot bring your daughter in here. One of our rules, you know.

(*The* COLONEL, *crossing to* R., *hands a glass to* MRS. BINGLEY.)

MRS. BINGLEY. I'm so sorry, Miss Philpott.

MISS PHILPOTT (*indulgently*). Doubtless she was anxious to enjoy her parents' society for as long as possible. (*To* JUDY.) Is that the reason of your presence, Bingley ?

JUDY. Yes, Miss Philpott.

MISS PHILPOTT. Well, wait outside for a while. Occupy your-self with something useful for a little. Can you contrive to do that ? (*She crosses above* JUDY *to the desk* L.)

JUDY. Yes, Miss Philpott.

(MISS PHILPOTT *pats* JUDY *as she passes her.* JUDY *exits* L.C., *hiding the glass.* MISS MANDRILL *taps her on the shoulder as she passes, and holds out her hand for the glass.*)

(*The* COLONEL *nudges* MRS. BINGLEY, *who rises and crosses* C. *to* MISS PHILPOTT, *who comes down* C.)

MRS. BINGLEY. I'm afraid we must be running away too, Miss Philpott. You'll be glad to see the last of us ! I know what a pest parents can be on speech day. (*She shakes hands.*) Good-bye. (*She crosses to the doors* R.)

MISS PHILPOTT. Good-bye, Mrs. Bingley. (*In* C.) Good-bye, Colonel. I fear I must return to my other guests. A head-mistress is never her own mistress on these occasions, is she ?

COLONEL (*vaguely*). No. I suppose she's somebody else's. (*He shakes hands.*) Good-bye.

(MISS PHILPOTT *takes her hand away. The* COLONEL *crosses to the door* R.)

MISS PHILPOTT (*coldly*). Miss Mandrill, will you see Colonel and Mrs. Bingley to the door ?

MISS MANDRILL (*with a stern eye on the* COLONEL). Immedi-ately, Miss Philpott.

(*There is a sudden turmoil outside the window, off* L.—*the voices of* MR. SMITHSON, EVE *and* JUDY *talking simultaneously.*)

SMITHSON		(C.) Come along, my girl ! I'm going to talk to Miss Philpott about you. You're just the one I was looking for, *etc.*
EVE	(*together*).	(R. *of* SMITHSON.) Let me go, I tell you ! How dare you, you nasty old man ! Kick him on the shins, Judy ! *etc.*
JUDY		(L. *of* SMITHSON.) Let her go, you old concrete-mixer ! You go on kicking his shins, Eve : I'll bite his ears ! *etc.*

(*They appear in the window, struggling.* MISS MANDRILL L.)

MISS PHILPOTT. What is this ?

MRS. BINGLEY. Good gracious ! It can't be——

COLONEL (*to* R. *of* MRS. BINGLEY). Good God—Eve as a scarlet runner, too !

SMITHSON. I am sorry to cause a disturbance, Miss Philpott, but I've brought this young lady along with me.

MISS PHILPOTT. So I observe, Mr. Smithson. What is the matter ?

EVE (*struggling*). Let me go !

JUDY. Let her go !

MISS PHILPOTT. Bingley, leave us at once. This is no scene for your eyes.

JUDY. No, Miss Philpott.

(JUDY *goes off* L.C. *quietly, kicking* SMITHSON *as she goes up.*)

MISS PHILPOTT. What is the meaning of this, Mr. Smithson ? Why have you brought one of my pupils here, in this summary manner ?

SMITHSON. Because I recognized her. She came running round a corner just now, and bumped straight into me. Nearly knocked the breath out of my body. But I was wise to her, and I held on to her.

MISS PHILPOTT (*calmly*). May I repeat my question ? Why have you brought her here ?

SMITHSON. I'll tell you that when you've sent for Mr. Budge.

MISS PHILPOTT. Mr. Budge ? (*Glancing at* MISS MANDRILL.)

SMITHSON. Yes. Ask her why. She knows ! The Bijou Cinema ! She got away with it last time——

COLONEL (*to* MRS. BINGLEY). How can anybody get away with a cinema ?

MRS. BINGLEY. Shut up !

SMITHSON. But last night I caught them with the goods. Send for Budge !

EVE. There's no need to send for Mr. Budge, Miss Philpott. I can explain everything.

MISS PHILPOTT. If these obscure innuendoes can be interpreted as meaning anything at all, Mr. Smithson, I think that the first person to send for is Rogers' guardian, who happens to be with us—Sir John Brent. (*She sits behind the desk.*)

SMITHSON (*a little taken aback*). Sir John Brent !

COLONEL. You're wrong there, Miss Philpott. Brent isn't her guar——

MRS. BINGLEY (*quickly*). Yes, he *is* here, dear. I saw him.

COLONEL. But she says——

MRS. BINGLEY (*quietly*). Shut *up* !

MISS PHILPOTT. Miss Mandrill, will you kindly find Sir John Brent ?

MISS MANDRILL. Yes, Miss Philpott.

(MISS MANDRILL *goes out by the windows* R.C.)

EVE (*steps* C.). There's no need to send for my—Sir John,

Miss Philpott. I can tell you the whole story. I was only having an algebra lesson.

(SMITHSON *laughs sarcastically*.)

MISS PHILPOTT (*rises*). Am I to understand that you were having an algebra lesson in a cinema ?
EVE. In the tea-room. We often do.
SMITHSON. I bet you do !
EVE. And this disgusting old snooper burst in on us——
SMITHSON. And found 'em kissing each other !
EVE. No, we weren't ! Budge was kissing me !

(SIR JOHN *and* MISS MANDRILL *have appeared in the window from* R.C. EVE *turns her back.* MISS MANDRILL *stands* R. *of the window.*)

MISS PHILPOTT (*bangs the desk*). One moment, please, here is Sir John.
MISS MANDRILL. This way, Sir John.
MISS PHILPOTT. I do not think you have met Mr. Samuel Smithson. Sir John Brent.
SIR JOHN (R. *of* SMITHSON). Good afternoon, Mr. Smithson.
SMITHSON (*rather deferentially*). Pleased to meet you, I'm sure.
SIR JOHN (*looking round the room*). Afternoon, Cynthia. Hallo, Ken !

(*His eye falls on* EVE, *who has turned her back. He stares.*)

SIR JOHN. Great heavens !

(*The* COLONEL *suddenly chokes and sits in the chair down* R. MRS. BINGLEY *hands him some passion fruit juice from the mantelpiece.*)

MISS PHILPOTT (*in front of the desk* L.). Your ward, Sir John, I am sorry to say——
SIR JOHN. What has my ward been doing, Miss Philpott ? Have you been getting into mischief—Ruby ?

(EVE *looks up at him suddenly. She realizes that he is playing up, and she must do the same. But he looks perfectly serious.*)

What is the charge, Miss Philpott ?
SMITHSON (*to* L. *of* SIR JOHN). Kissing ! Kissing in the Bijou Cinema with a person called Budge.
EVE (*opposite* SMITHSON). I wasn't ! I won't listen to any more of this ! I'm going !
SIR JOHN (*quietly, detaining her with a hand on her arm*). Suppose we allow Miss Philpott to conduct this inquiry, Mr. Smithson.
MISS PHILPOTT. I fear Mr. Smithson's charges are correct in substance if not in detail, Sir John. Ruby has admitted as much.
SIR JOHN. In that case we need hardly prolong this dis-

cussion, need we ?   Ruby, you had better come home with me, for the rest of the afternoon.

EVE.   For the rest ?   For ever !

SIR JOHN.   That is for me to decide.

SMITHSON.   But I say, aren't we going to have a real show-down ?   I've taken a lot of trouble over this case.   You ask my Hilda !

SIR JOHN (*ignoring him*).   I'm sorry this should have happened, Miss Philpott.

MISS PHILPOTT.   So am I, Sir John.   It may mean expulsion.

SIR JOHN.   I should not like to think that my own—h'm—ward had been expelled from school.   The fault, I feel, is possibly mine. Ruby here is impulsive, a little flighty perhaps ; a trifle susceptible, shall we say ?   I should have supervised her young life more carefully.   Yes, it is my fault !

MISS PHILPOTT.   Is it not rather the fault of Lady Brent ? Surely that was her province !

(SMITHSON *crosses up* L. *and places his hat on the desk.*   COLONEL BINGLEY *chokes again.   He looks positively apoplectic.*)

SIR JOHN.   No, Miss Philpott ; there I join issue with you. My wife is not to blame.   You have never met her, I think.

MISS PHILPOTT.   No !   I have not had that pleasure.

SIR JOHN.   Well, she is very young.   She and Ruby are almost like sisters.   Sometimes I am tempted to feel that one is as foolish as the other.   Isn't that so, Ruby ?

(EVE *looks up at him and smiles.*   MRS. BINGLEY *again quickly soothes her husband.*)

Now, if I may, I should like to have a chat with Mr. Budge. Before deciding upon what disciplinary action I must take with my ward, I must hear his version of the matter.   I suppose I shall find him in the garden ?   (*To the window.*)

EVE (*stopping him*).   There's no need !

MISS PHILPOTT.   Sit down, Rogers.

(EVE *sits on the stool* R.C.)

Miss Mandrill will accompany you.   Before I leave you, may I bring up one other point.   It refers to Ruby's home-life.

SIR JOHN.   Ruby's home-life.   Certainly.

MISS PHILPOTT.   Your answer may explain much, even condone much.   How does Ruby spend her evenings ?   I ask because her work in the morning is frequently ill-prepared. At times she gives me the impression of not having had sufficient sleep.

SIR JOHN.   I must look into this.

MISS PHILPOTT.   About what time does she usually go to bed ?

SIR JOHN.   About the same time as my wife.

MISS PHILPOTT. I think she should go earlier.

SIR JOHN (*looks at* EVE). I will speak to my wife about it.

MISS MANDRILL (*to* L.C. *of the window*). Are you ready, Sir John ?

SIR JOHN (*going up to the window*). Perfectly.

MISS MANDRILL. He will probably be in the tea tent. He usually is.

(*They both exit by the windows* R.C.)

MISS PHILPOTT (*to* MRS. BINGLEY, *who has been trying to edge over to* EVE). Now, Mrs. Bingley, I will show you out myself. Are you coming, Mr. Smithson ? (*She crosses above the desk and picks up her mortar-board and a book.*)

SMITHSON. I'm going to have a talk with my Hilda.

(*He crosses to the window and exits* R.C.)

MISS PHILPOTT. I see. (*She crosses to* EVE.) Compose yourself with a book, Rogers, until your guardian returns. (*She hands the book.*)

EVE. Yes, Miss Philpott.

MISS PHILPOTT. Come along, Mrs. Bingley.

(*They both exit down* R. *The* COLONEL *lingers for a moment, then tiptoes over to* EVE. *She turns suddenly. He starts violently and hurries out.*)

(EVE *throws the book on the settee.* JUDY *appears outside the window* L. *peeping round the corner, then coming down* C.)

JUDY. All over ? Blood wiped up and everything ?

EVE. I'm not sure yet. I haven't had a chance to talk to Jack.

JUDY. I don't envy you when you do, my child. The beans are spilled, all right. No use in doing in Hilda Smithson now. There's nothing left to spill. I should have loved to cosh her, all the same.

EVE. Nothing left to spill ? Isn't there ? Judy, listen. (*She crosses to* R. *of* JUDY.) Where's Hilda Smithson now ?

JUDY. I think she's gone to draw a gas-mask. She's in that gas parade. Why ?

EVE. The beans aren't spilled ! They're only half spilled, and it's the important half that isn't. Philpott and Smithson know all about Ruby Rogers and Budge. But do they know that I am a married woman—a respectable British matron ?

JUDY. No !

EVE. And they mustn't ! Nobody must ! Think of the Sunday papers ! " Titled surgeon's bride steals back to school ! "

JUDY. Back to pinafores and pigtails !

EVE. Funny jokes from Lord Castlerosse !

JUDY. Tears from Godfrey Winn !

EVE. I don't know what Jack's going to do to me for this, but
he's been a brick so far. He saved my face, and now I'm going to
save his ! (*Going up* C.) Come on.

JUDY (*following*). What are we going to do ?

EVE. Find Hilda before she meets her filthy father, and bump
her off.

JUDY. But she'll be missed at the gas parade.

EVE. No she won't ! Leave it to me !

(*They both go up to the window* C. *and look off* R.)

Jack and the Mandrill—— !

JUDY. This way, through the study ! Come on.

(*Both exit through the door* L.)

(MISS MANDRILL *and* SIR JOHN *enter through the window from* R.C.)

MISS MANDRILL. I am so sorry not to have found Mr. Budge
for you, Sir John.

SIR JOHN. Anyway, I've had the pleasure of meeting you,
Miss Mandrill. Someone was singing your praises to me only a
few moments ago.

MISS MANDRILL. Indeed, Sir John ! Who ?

SIR JOHN. Colonel Bingley. He said I must see you at any
cost.

MISS MANDRILL. About what ?

SIR JOHN. Oh, nothing. Just see you—meet you. That was
all.

MISS MANDRILL (*simpering*). Oh, Sir John. Delightful,
delightful. But I'm afraid we must postpone all this. I have a
favour to ask of you. I wonder if you'd be so kind as to present
the efficiency badges to the Members of our A.R.P. contingent,
and perhaps address an individual word of congratulation to
each ?

SIR JOHN. I shall be delighted.

MISS MANDRILL. There are only four of them. I must go and
see if they are mustered.

(*Exit down* L.)

SIR JOHN (*to below the desk, placing his hat on the desk*). Mus-
tard ! Precisely !

(*Enter* BUDGE *from the door down* R.)

BUDGE. Sir John Brent ?

SIR JOHN. Yes.

BUDGE. My name is Mervyn Budge. I wonder if I could
speak to you for a moment, sir.

SIR JOHN. Certainly.

BUDGE (*he crosses to* R.C. *He has evidently rehearsed the scene*). Sir, I may as well come to the point at once.

SIR JOHN. Always a praiseworthy habit. What is the point ?

BUDGE. I wish to make formal application for your ward's hand in marriage.

SIR JOHN (*staring. He sits down* R. *of the desk suddenly*). You are referring, I presume—to—er—Miss Ruby Rogers ?

BUDGE. Yes. Have you got some more wards ?

SIR JOHN. God forbid. In fact, I—— How long have you known Miss Rogers ?

BUDGE. A fortnight !

SIR JOHN. Isn't that rather a short acquaintance ? Won't you sit down ?

(BUDGE *sits on the stool* R.C.)

Aren't we rushing our fences a little ?

BUDGE. Yes, sir ; but the fact is, a bit of an emergency has cropped up. Do you know a perisher—a person—named Smithson ? Samuel Smithson, I think his disgusting christian name is.

SIR JOHN. I have met him.

BUDGE. He is the father of one of the girls in this school——

SIR JOHN. So I have gathered.

BUDGE. And he's chock full of moral uplift. Oh yes. He doesn't approve of public demonstrations of affection——

SIR JOHN (*absently*). However legitimate. I beg your pardon ! Go on.

BUDGE. In fact, he once reported a Tadworthy girl to Miss Philpott for something of that kind. Now he's on the job again. The other evening he slid into a favourite stamping-ground of his —the Bijou Cinema, in Upper Baker Street——

SIR JOHN. And found you and my ward in the tea-room.

BUDGE. Yes.

SIR JOHN. What were you doing ?

BUDGE. Well, at the moment I was kissing her—in a respectful way, of course. You see, I thought we were alone.

SIR JOHN. I believe you. And Mr. Smithson pounced ?

BUDGE. Pounced is the word, sir.

SIR JOHN. What did he do ?

BUDGE. After a little back-chat with me, he asked your ward her name.

SIR JOHN. As a matter of idle curiosity, what name did she give ?

BUDGE. She said her name was Snow White.

SIR JOHN. Which Mr. Smithson found unconvincing ?

BUDGE. Yes. He blew up, and said he was going to report us both to Miss Philpott.

SIR JOHN. Wasn't that rather overstepping the bounds of officiousness ? Is your private life any affair of Miss Philpott's ?

BUDGE. Mine, no. But your ward, sir ? He recognized her as a member of the School.

SIR JOHN. As a member of the school. Go on.

BUDGE. Even though she was not wearing the School uniform.

SIR JOHN. Even though she—— (*Suddenly.*) Tell me—has she been wearing the School uniform for long ?

BUDGE. Ever since she came here, I suppose, sir.

SIR JOHN. Of course—of course. Let me see ; how long is that ?

BUDGE. I'm not sure, sir. She only comes to me for private coaching, you see.

SIR JOHN (*staring at him*). Private coaching ?

BUDGE. Yes ; in mathematics—for the Higher Certificate——

SIR JOHN. If you will excuse me, I will drink a glass of Kia-Ora. (*He rises and helps himself to a glass of Kia-Ora from the table up R. and returns to C.*) And you do your private coaching in cinema tea-rooms ? (C.)

BUDGE. Yes ; it was unavoidable. Your ward told me that there was no suitable accommodation for her at home. You were invariably in the consulting-room, she said, and Lady Brent was in and out of the drawing-room.

(SIR JOHN *suddenly chuckles, then roars with laughter.*)

SIR JOHN (*to above the desk*). In and out. How good that is ! Tell me more !

BUDGE (*smiling*). I think you have tumbled to the same idea as I have, sir.

SIR JOHN. What is that ?

BUDGE (*rises, crosses C. to the chair R. of the desk*). Do you know what I think, sir ? These cinema meetings, and so on, were just an excuse—to keep you from finding out that she was coming to me for coaching. She wanted to spring that Higher Certificate on you as a big surprise !

SIR JOHN. Higher Certificate ! A big surprise ! And that is all ?

BUDGE. I'm certain of it, sir. That must be the real reason. From certain little things she let drop——

SIR JOHN. What sort of little things ?

BUDGE. Little odd things about you—funny little affectionate things. She's very fond of you, sir. It has been rather touching sometimes.

SIR JOHN. Has it ? (*He smiles.*) Does she refer to Lady Brent at all ?

BUDGE. No. (*He sits R. of the desk.*) She doesn't seem to think so much of her. (*Hastily.*) I mean, not so much *about* her. Have I said something stupid ? (*Rising.*)

SIR JOHN (*puts him back*). On the contrary. Well, let's get back to business. You wish to marry her ?

BUDGE. I am willing to marry her.

SIR JOHN. Only willing ? What the devil do you mean ?

BUDGE. Her honour, sir.

SIR JOHN. Her what ?

BUDGE. Her reputation.

(SIR JOHN *sits behind the desk*.)

That fellow Smithson—he's shown us up—and that means the sack for her—doesn't it, sir ?

SIR JOHN. I'm inclined to concur in your view.

BUDGE. Now perhaps you see the idea ? If Ruby—if Miss Rogers and I were able to stand up before a whole crowd and announce our engagement officially, that would knock Smithson's end in, wouldn't it ?

SIR JOHN. For the moment, certainly. But—are you suggesting that this engagement should only be a fake—a blind ?

BUDGE. Oh no, sir. I'm responsible for this mess ; I'm prepared to go through with it.

SIR JOHN (*angrily*). Damn it all, do you mean to sit there and tell me you don't want to marry my wi—ward ?

BUDGE. Well, sir, that's what I don't quite know. It's all very odd. (*He pulls up a chair*.) When first I set eyes on her a fortnight ago, sitting at her desk in school, wearing the School uniform, I merely said to myself that she was the most attractive girl in the whole outfit.

SIR JOHN. Which, of course, she was.

BUDGE. Far and away. Far and away. But that was all there was to it. Nothing more. I mean—she looked such a kid !

SIR JOHN. I know, old man, I know ! Go on.

BUDGE. But when she changed her clothes and did herself up, and when I found myself alone with her—looking like twenty-three or four—the loveliest thing—I got carried away.

SIR JOHN. So did I. Yes ?

BUDGE (*eagerly*). You know—the set of her head, the grace of her carriage, the unconscious child-like beauty of her attitudes——

SIR JOHN (*eagerly*). Yes—yes !

BUDGE. And so on and so forth—well, they took my breath away, as it were. You understand ?

SIR JOHN. Quite ! Quite !

BUDGE. But that was all there was to it. Next morning when I saw her again, in her schoolgirl kit, with her flat heels and shiny little nose, I sort of recovered my balance again.

SIR JOHN. That was fortunate.

BUDGE. Yes, sir, wasn't it ? (*Rising, he crosses round* C. *to above the chair*.) And then I discovered she was a liar as well !

SIR JOHN. She's always telling lies, especially to people she loves. What particular lie did she tell you ?

BUDGE. She said she was married and had a title.

SIR JOHN. Did she ? The little swank ! And so, Mr. Budge, I take it that you don't love her ?

BUDGE. I don't see how I can, sir, or I suppose I'd always feel the same about her, whatever she wore and however she looked.

SIR JOHN. You're dead right. You would.

BUDGE. But I won't allow that to make any difference, sir. My offer still holds good.

SIR JOHN (*rising*). And it is declined.

BUDGE (*eagerly*). You mean that, sir ?

SIR JOHN. I do. (*Slapping him on the shoulder*.) My dear fellow, you have behaved splendidly ! You are a most chivalrous English gentleman——

BUDGE (*modestly*). Oh, not at all !

SIR JOHN. But you shall make no more sacrifices on her behalf. Leave the matter entirely to me. I will settle with this Smithson ; and I will settle with my ward. Good-bye, and God bless you ! God bless everybody ! (*He impels him towards the door*.)

BUDGE. You're not annoyed with me, sir ?

SIR JOHN. Annoyed ? My dear fellow, I never felt so affectionate towards anybody in my life. (*He takes a carnation from his buttonhole and puts it into Budge's*.) Get out, for pity's sake, get out !

(*He pushes* BUDGE *off* R., *quite bewildered.* SIR JOHN *crosses to above the desk* L., *executing a high kick on the way. He picks up his glass of Kia-Ora and is about to drink, but changes his mind and pours the contents into a pot-pourri jar on the desk.* MISS MANDRILL *enters down* L.)

Ah, Miss Mandrill ! Nothing can keep us apart !

MISS MANDRILL. Oh, Sir John ! (*Handing him the badges*.) Here are the badges. Are you ready ?

SIR JOHN. Ready for anything !

MISS MANDRILL. I will call each girl's name in turn. (*As she crosses to the door* R.) Party, *Atten-tion !*

(*Exit* MISS MANDRILL *down* R. *The girls mark time off stage*.)

(JUDY *enters hurriedly from the window* L.C., *goes to* SIR JOHN *and takes his handkerchief out of his pocket*.)

JUDY. Coast clear ? Good ! I want a big handkerchief.

SIR JOHN. Here, I say, stop that ! What do you want it for ?

JUDY (*chanting and dancing*). Somebody's nose is bleeding !
Somebody's nose is bleeding !

SIR JOHN. Whose ?

JUDY (*up to* C.). Just one of my fellow pupils. So long !

(*Exit* JUDY *by the windows* L.C.)

(MISS MANDRILL *enters, and stands above the door* R. *She clicks
her heels and comes to attention.*)

MISS MANDRILL. Party, quick march ! (*She reads out their
names as they enter, each wearing a gas-mask.*) Joan Timpson.
Amy Battersby. Claire Westbrook. Hilda Smithson.

(SIR JOHN *hands each a badge in turn, saying a few words to each :
No.* 1. " Congratulations." TIMPSON *answers :* " Thank you
very much." *No.* 2. " Hearty congratulations." *No.* 3.
" Those masks must be very hot. I wish I could see your
face." *No.* 4. " You look so efficient." *As each girl receives
her badge, she exits through the window to* R.C. *As the last one
exits,* SIR JOHN *recognizes her to be* EVE, *runs after her and brings
her back—down* C. *and stands laughing at her.*)

SIR JOHN. Eve Angela Duval Brent !

(*She pulls off her mask angrily.*)

EVE. How did you know it was me with that thing on ?

SIR JOHN. I can recognize you from any angle.   " The set of
her head—the grace of her carriage—the unconscious child-like
beauty of her attitudes "— And so on, and so forth. That's a
quotation, by the way, from one of our rising mathematicians
and romanticists. Excuse me, but I'm feeling slightly mad.
(*He crosses* R. *to the stool and sits.*)

EVE. With what ?

SIR JOHN. Relief ! Joy ! Felicity !

EVE (*crosses to the same stool and kneels on the end*). You
mean this isn't the end of everything ?

SIR JOHN. I'm not quite sure yet. How long has this nonsense been going on ?

EVE. What nonsense ?

SIR JOHN. Your membership of this select establishment.

EVE. Do you remember the night when you asked me to
come out on a party with you—for the first time, really—and
you put me off at the last minute to go to the hospital, or something ?

SIR JOHN. I do.

EVE. That was the night Ruby Rogers was born. I handed
her over to Judy, and she's been coming here to school every
day, except on half-holidays, since the middle of May.

SIR JOHN. I see.

Eve (*eagerly*). Of course it didn't prevent you and me from being together in the evenings—and things like that, *did* it ?

Sir John. And how long did you propose to pursue this career of duplicity ?

Eve. Till I got that Higher Certificate !

Sir John. And that's all ?

Eve (*with an effort*). No. (*She sits.*) I've got to be honest. There's a mathematical master called——

Sir John. Perhaps I can finish it for you. (*He rises, crosses* L.C. *in front of the desk.*) But before I do, I want to consult you about something ; women are always so infallibly right in their instincts about such matters. (*Solemnly.*) I've just been having an interview with a young man, who has made a formal proposal for the hand of our ward, little Ruby.

(Eve *stares at him.*)

Does that surprise you ? Did you know anything about this ?

Eve. Yes, I knew something about it.

Sir John. Have you met him at all ?

Eve (*adopting his serious tone*). Occasionally, dear.

Sir John. He seemed a nice steady young fellow. What do you think ? Do you happen to know how the child feels about him ?

(*A little pause.*)

Eve. She doesn't care for him one little bit.

Sir John. You are very positive. Why ?

Eve. Because she's madly in love with somebody else.

Sir John. Ah, then we need think no more about it.

Eve. But we must !

Sir John. Why ?

Eve (*rises*). It's a married man she's in love with !

Sir John. Good gracious ! Has this been going on for long ?

Eve (*crosses to* Sir John). Ever since the day she married him. (*She puts her arms round his neck and they embrace.*) Tell me. Did Mr. Budge really want to marry me ?

Sir John. No. He was merely willing to—and that's one in the eye for you, my cherub. Apparently he only loves you when you're dressed as a grown-up woman ; as a flat-heeled school-girl you don't appeal to him at all. And that's where he differs from me. (*He kisses her.*)

Eve. Still, I wish that flat-heeled schoolgirl could have got that Higher Certificate for you.

Sir John. We'll take it as signed. We'll get Judy to sign it.

(*Enter* Judy *from the french windows* L.C. *She comes down* C.)

Sir John. Go away !

JUDY. Here is the news, and this is Julia Bingley spilling it. They've found the body!

SIR JOHN. What?

JUDY. The deceased—the remains! In the potting-shed! Hilda Smithson, bound hand and foot, smothered in gore, and yowling for help! Don't stand there necking! Smithson's on your track.

SIR JOHN. Smithson the Avenger! Does he know all?

JUDY. He knows one of us gave his daughter a bloody nose.

SIR JOHN. Not me. I'm as pure as driven snow.

JUDY. Oh! Are you? Hilda's legs were tied together with a pocket handkerchief, and the Mandrill found your name on it. (*She crosses up to the window.*) Scram!

(*Exit* JUDY *through the french windows up* L.C.)

(*Music off stage starts playing " Spread A Little Happiness " from " Mr. Cinders."*)

SIR JOHN. Shall we be moving, your Ladyship?

EVE. Are we really going to bolt?

SIR JOHN. It seems the only thing to do at the moment. Lady Brent, your arm. (*He crosses round to up* C.) Farewell to that remarkable woman Euphemia Tadworthy—and her Foundation. (*Pointing to the picture over the fireplace,* R.C.) By the way. What are we going to do with little Ruby now?

EVE (L.C.). I know: we'll send her abroad to a finishing school, and get her out of the way.

SIR JOHN. I can think of a better one than that. I'll take her abroad myself. We need a holiday, both of us.

EVE. All three of us! Where shall we go?

SIR JOHN. Paris? Buda Pesth?

EVE. Venice?

SIR JOHN. Venice! Carried unanimously!

(*The music swells louder. They exit through the french windows* C., *then hurry out* L.C.)

CURTAIN.

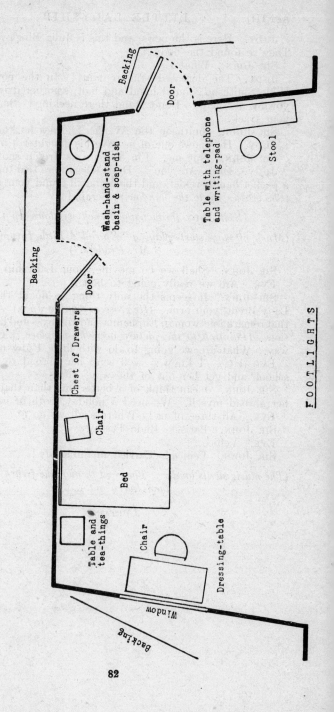

ACT I sc. 1

FOOTLIGHTS

ACT I sc. 1A

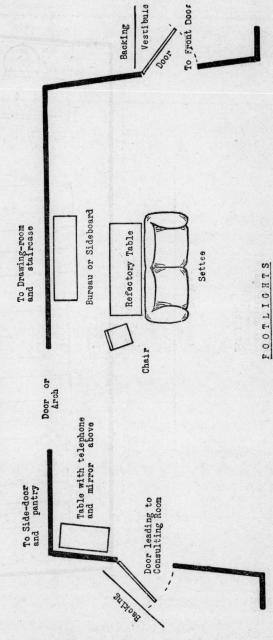

Backing

Vestibule

Door

To Front Door

To Drawing-room
and staircase

Bureau or Sideboard

Refectory Table

Settee

Chair

Backing

Door or Arch

Table with telephone
and mirror above

To Side-door
and pantry

Door leading to
Consulting Room

Backing

FOOTLIGHTS

83

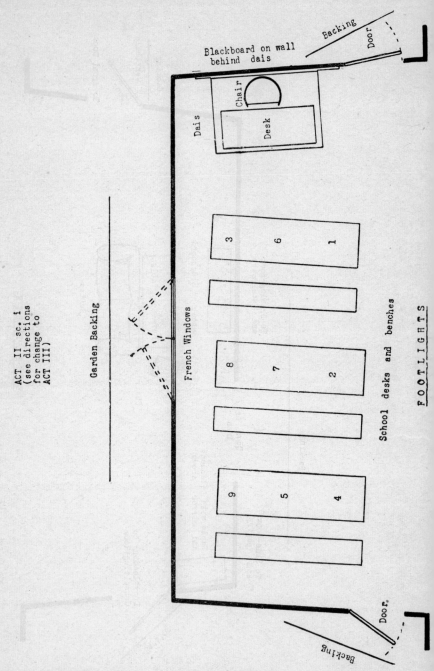

ACT II sc. 1
(see directions
for change to
ACT III)

Garden Backing

French Windows

Blackboard on wall
behind dais

Backing

Door

Chair

Dais

Desk

3 6 1

8 7 2

9 5 4

School desks and benches

Door

Backing

FOOTLIGHTS

If there are sufficient girls, another desk for two can be placed between
the R. wall and desks 4 5 9 for the full complement of eleven pupils.

84